T0149151

JETTY JEWELS INC.
LOS ANGELES

CONQUERING LIFE'S STAGE FRIGHT

THREE STEPS TO TOP PERFORMANCE

BY MARK SCHULMAN

This book is a must-read for anyone who's ever stressed about a toast at a wedding, a presentation at work, a sales pitch or even late night karaoke with friends. Through first-hand experience, interviews and anecdotes, Mark Schulman provides unparalleled insight into the mindset and skill set required to break through the barriers and nerves that are present for even the most skilled performers. *Conquering Life's Stage Fright* presents a clear path from anxiety to confidence for anyone seeking to unleash their full potential on stage, in the workplace and in everyday life.

LEIGH GALLAGHER Assistant Managing Editor, *FORTUNE*, Author *"The End of the Suburbs"*

Mark Schulman takes "fake it till you make it' to a whole new level. As a professional drummer for some of the world's most iconic musical artists, he's understandably had more than his fair share of stage fright. However, his revealing self-help book—which is made even juicier with a dozen celebrity-peppered examples— describes the tie that binds us all as humans: anxiety. Usually associated with job interviews and public speaking, he proves that everyone from rockstars and pro athletes, to firefighters and heart surgeons, suffers from a ubiquitous sense of stage fright. His "three Cs" method for overcoming this feeling -- clarity, capability, and confidence—can turn any nerve-breaking situation into an opportunity for success. His introspective book is a how-to guide for channeling your inner rockstar.

FELLOW CONQUERORS

MARC CENEDELLA Founder and Executive Chairman, TheLadders

Through experience, interviews, and anecdotes, Mark Schulman provides insight into the mindset and skill sets that can be used to break through the barriers to success and beyond. *Conquering Life's Stage Fright* can help with expanding the human potential in the workplace as well as achieving greater purpose and happiness in life itself.

TONY HSIEH NY Times Best Selling Author *"Delivering Happiness"* CEO of Zappos.com

This is a world-class talent with a world-class message.

DR. JIM SAMUELS Author *"Re-Mind Yourself"*

Mark Schulman has 'schooled' hundreds of my university leadership students with a passionate, engaging and revelatory presentation of the Three Cs. This book will do for you what it did for them, ROCK their world!

DR. RONDA BEAMAN Professor of Practice, Orfalea College of Business, California Polytechnic University

Okay, so who has more legit cred on how to conquer life's stage fright than the dude who's performed in front of a billion people worldwide? When every gig feels like an audition, only Mark Schulman in this fresh, approachable in-your-face book, equips you to harness the best of "what's in here" to bring your absolute unbridled best to everyone and everything "out there."

DR. PAUL STOLTZ Best Selling Author *"Adversity Quotient"* CEO Peak Learning

Mark hits all the right marks with his book! When he does a speaking presentation, He takes time to customize his program for each audience. His energy is infectious and his information valuable. He really makes each person in the audience feel like he is talking to them individually. Mark is interactive, has high energy and he will not disappoint!

MAUREEN BROOKS President, Brooks International Speakers and Entertainment Bureau

Mark is a lovecat; he became the greatest so he could give it away. Take it from me, a musician has a unique view of the world that is useful to anyone that has ever created, sold or destroyed something.

TIM SANDERS Chief Solutions Officer, YAHOO! Best Selling Author *"Love is the Killer App"*

Mark Schulman is the quintessential consummate pro; he can do anything and everything and he does so with a smile on his face and a wonderful, nurturing heart. His infectious positive attitude is a huge asset to all those around him. Putting Mark in a room or a stage or a studio is a guarantee that not only will the communication and music be on the very highest order, but that all those involved in the project will be relaxed, filled with confidence and have a great time. He's like a walking ray of sunshine. Oh, and he plays his ASS off too!

DAVE KOZ Grammy Winning Artist, Producer Beverly Hills, CA

SET LIST

FOREWORD

LEIGH GALLAGHER

Managing Editor,
FORTUNE magazine,
Author *"The End of the
Suburbs"*

On the surface, Mark Schulman and I make an odd pair. Mark is a rock star of the highest order—a 25-year, world-class, touring drummer, a veteran of the road with some of the biggest names in rock, from P!NK to Foreigner to Cher to Billy Idol. He looks the part—piercings, tattoos, soul patch, rocker hair, rocker jewelry and all. I'm a financial journalist who wears suits and pumps to work, subscribes to The Wall Street Journal and is more prone to talking about the GDP or the moves of the Federal Reserve than the head-banging magic of a rare Led Zeppelin bootleg (though I do happen to be a Led Zeppelin fan).

And yet we are both performers, Mark in front of hundreds of thousands at a time—nearly a billion people to date—and me, as part of my role at *Fortune*, often in front of a television camera on shows such as Morning Joe or CBS This Morning that beam out to millions. The topic and nature of our performances could not be more different: Mark rocks out for hours at a time; I sit in on television roundtables and discuss where the economy is headed. Mark sweats up a storm and plays a drum battle with P!NK on stage; the craziest thing I've ever done on air is admit my personal political leanings.

But Mark and I share two big things in common: nerves and how to break them.

I first met Mark a few years ago when he was looking to talk to people in the business community about their experiences conquering stage fright. When we first spoke over the phone, I liked him right away; Mark is relentlessly upbeat, friendly and gregarious and contagiously optimistic. He's also thoughtful and insightful. He'd done all his homework on me, and he mentioned a few stories I'd written. He's a loyal Morning Joe watcher, so we talked about that, too.

But I was also struck by his topic, conquering stage fright. I had been going on television for years, yet I still found myself some- times hit with nerves just before going on air. I had recently begun to speak in public more regularly, often as a keynote speaker in front of large audiences, and it was a new format I was still getting used to. I was happy to share with Mark what I'd learned over the years from my experience and, after hearing more about the kinds of people Mark was talking to, to learn from others. But I had one question: It's one thing for me or even accomplished CEOs and other high-profile figures to get nervous, but did rock stars really get stage fright?

Turns out the answer is yes, as evidenced by the heart-pounding, nerve-wracking anecdote Mark relays in the first few pages of this book. It was that experience that led Mark to vow to conquering that stage fright into submission. Fortunately for the rest of us, he did just that, with tremendous success—and he's now willing to share the rituals, habits and tips that let him do it.

And who can't benefit from those lessons? It's an oft-cited fact that almost everyone's No. 1 fear is public speaking—and these days, everyone is a public speaker of some kind. Whether it's a high-profile gig like stepping up to a podium on a stage or doing a television interview, or something more everyday, like giving a toast, making a presentation, running a race, singing karaoke, going on a job interview or even having an important family discussion, we're all public performers these days—and every one of these situations has the potential to be busted by nerves. And while a little bit of nervousness can be a good thing, with a jolt of energy that can actually lead to better performances, debilitating nerves— which as *Conquering Life's Stage Fright* shows afflict even the most successful people—are not. Debilitating nerves mean you can be really, really ready and still fail. With *Conquering Life's Stage Fright*, Mark gives us a lively, tip-filled playbook for eviscerating these fears. He structures the book around three main pillars—clarity, capability and confidence—but the magic of Nerve Breakers is that Mark not only shares his own experience conquering fear, but talks to people from all walks about how they broke free of theirs as well. We learn, for example, from Zappos CEO Tony Hsieh not to memorize but to speak passionately from the heart; from pro surfer Garrett McNamara to oxygenate before a big, daunting task; and from Prodigal Sun of the Wu-Tang Clan to befriend the audience. (Did you ever think you'd be getting business tips from the Wu-Tang Clan? Me either.)

There are moving lessons from the first blind man to climb Mount Everest, from a heart surgeon who conquered his nerves to save lives under pressure, even from an astronaut, Alan Bean. There is some simple advice, too, from an online sales executive who throws a Led Zeppelin playlist on in his car right before a presentation to get pumped up. (I second that idea.)

Woven throughout these tips are entertaining anecdotes from some of the biggest names in the business. Jeremy Piven recalls how an early experience bombing in a performance at summer camp instilled in him a near-religious dedication to preparation. Stewart Copeland recalls how the Police's first arena gig at Madison Square Garden was almost derailed when the bass drum head broke mid-performance. And, of course, there are tales from Mark's own years on the road, like the epiphany he had when he was about to play "Feels Like the First Time" for what felt like the 301st time or the "gratitude circles" the P!NK band has just before each show that cause the group's energy level to spike in the critical moments just before taking the stage.

There are many other practical insights on public speaking, too—why speaking in front of 50 people is more difficult than speaking in front of 2,000, the importance of visualization and even how to best ace a job interview (including what might be the best response to that tricky what-is-your-current-compensation question that I have ever heard, courtesy of TheLadders.com CEO Marc Cenedella).

Despite having appeared on television and on stage for years, I found myself taking notes the entire time I was reading *Conquering Life's Stage Fright*. This is a book that can help anyone who's looking to gain an edge in their public speaking and even in their day-to-day communication, whether it's your first or 100th time stepping out in front of a group. But it's also a lively, engaging read. *Conquering Life's Stage Fright* is about lessons, but it's not preachy. It's a guide to self-improvement, but it's not at all "self-help-y." It's a rollicking, entertaining book filled with practical, usable tips on how to break through one of the biggest blocks in every one of us—delivered by a real-life, bona fide rock star. Through engaging interviews and in his spirited, inimitably optimistic voice, Mark's clear writing, potent ideas and life-changing lessons shine through—and that's a good thing for the rock star in all of us.

Leigh Gallagher
New York, NY

PROLOGUE

I'm a drummer. That's who I am—it has been since before I can remember. Turning that into a career hasn't always been easy, though it's generally been a lot of fun.

Not always. There were some big hurdles early on, and later some profound experiences, that shaped my attitudes, affected my behavior and altered the consequences of my life. Twenty-odd years ago, I experienced a moment of such anxiety that I couldn't judge my internal sense of time, find my rhythm or even breathe—despite years of building up to that moment.

The Audition

It's 1989. I've just finished my first world tour as drummer for R&B artist Brenda Russell, primarily as the opening act for Billy Ocean. I'm recovering at home when the call comes. My friend, singer-songwriter Dan Reed, who's well connected in the biz and friendly with guys from Journey, has learned that some of the band's über-members are putting together a super-group with singer John Waite. He thinks I should audition.

It's The Beatles-size gig I've dreamed of since I was kid. Dan gives me the contact number, and I'm giddy. I thank him profusely and immediately call the manager. I'm intimidated and excited, a cocktail of energy that I hope he interprets as somewhat professional. He gives me a day, time and place for an audition the following week.

Now, my experience on the world stage isn't…robust. I played the world tour with Brenda, but I didn't have to audition for that job—my old friend, Armand Grimaldi, recommended me, and I just played well enough to keep it. Despite this, here I am, a contender for this mega gig, Bad English. I fantasize about playing in a band with some of the most successful musicians in pop-rock history, a band that has the entire industry buzzing, and a band with carte blanche in the form of an absurd record deal. This audition will be my defining moment.

I've been on big stages for the last six months, so I know that I can play with big energy. I'm a Journey and John Waite fan; I'm familiar with what these artists have done. So, I prepare by listening to their music and practicing grooves and rock licks in front of a mirror.

I've been working out like a beast; I feel strong and sexy. I take my girl-friend, Michelle, shopping, and we find some seriously cool rock threads for my perfect visual presentation. I get my long, curly, dyed-blonde hair trimmed and make sure my supply of Aqua Net cement-hold hair spray is stocked up. I shine my boots and jewelry. I'm ready.

The morning of the audition I'm excited—and a bit nervous. I figure it's just performance anxiety, the kind that happens all the time that no one takes too seriously. There are butterflies in my belly all morning, but it feels totally appropriate and I'm not concerned. At noon, I kiss Michelle, get in my van and blast off from Venice to North Hollywood and Leeds Rehearsal, the coolest practice spot in NoHo.

As I drive, I reflect on the magnitude of the gig and how much it means to me. I've attached a lot to the outcome, and the physical effects of anxiety start taking hold. I'm sweating. My heart is pounding. I get anxious about being anxious, which exacerbates everything. I try to focus on drumming and music, but my head's in a haze. I'm queasy. "Calm down," I repeat to myself. But I can't control it. I wonder if it's an anxiety attack.

I get to Leeds and park in back. I'm a wreck. I take a few deep breaths, start observing my own behavior and practice some techniques I've learned over the years. I run an exercise called a freedom flow. "I'm free to get this gig. I'm free not to get this gig. I'm free to totally mess up this audition. I'm free to not totally mess up this audition." I repeat this until I start to release. The haze lifts. The nervousness feels manageable.

I enter the rehearsal studio lobby and walk into the men's room. My energy has turned from dull to fidgety. I look in the mirror, splash some water on my face and, like Roy Scheider in *All That Jazz*, I say, "It's show time, folks!"

I walk down the corridor to Studio A, see all the signed posters of famous musicians and fantasize about being at a relaxed photo shoot and not at this agonizing audition. I force a smile, pop open the door and see the iconic rockers I've only ever seen in photos.

Guitarist Neal Schon is super-tan and shorter than I thought. He extends his hand. Singer John Waite is slender—a perfectly coiffed rocker; he coolly nods hello. Bassist Ricky Phillips is warm, an ally, and keyboardist Jonathan Cain is formal and standoffish, like a businessman at a seminar. (Years later, Jonathan and I laughed about this audition, as our bands, Foreigner and Journey, toured the world together. He doesn't even remember it, and it was one of the defining experiences of my life—go figure!)

I sit behind the rented drum kit, my hands so sweaty that the tech has to make all the adjustments for me. I'm not paying much attention to detail. I wonder how many other drummers these rock stars have met. I wonder what it must be like to go through a haystack of players looking for a shiny needle.

I'm actually a bit numb, which is a welcome reprieve from the butterflies that had metamorphosed into bats in my stomach. The guys get in position, and Jonathan tells me we'll jam on one of their song ideas. They play a bit without me as a preview. I nod my head in a groovy drummer way.

I smack a few drums and cymbals to check the gear one last time. I force another smile and take a deep breath. Jonathan counts it off, and I blast into the song with everything I have, and, at that point, I'm not even sure what is going on. I try to concentrate, but I feel totally alien on the drums. I'm sure my face looks pained. I look up at Ricky, and he gives me the bass-player-funky-face-of-approval. That helps, and I start to feel the groove. I feel empowered and calmer, like myself.

Suddenly, like a needle ripped off a record, Jonathan stops the band. I cringe. I know it. He looks at me, disappointed, and says, "Mark, you're rushing."

Ouch!

I'm embarrassed. I remember that long, long, really long moment with clarity: the blood rushing out of my face, my stomach turning, seeing John Waite look away as I search for some support. Neal plays a blazing riff, and instead of enjoying it, I see it as intimidation.

I try to smile, adjust my drum stool, stutter an apology and ask Jonathan to count off the tune. At this point I don't even trust myself to do that. I try really hard to find my groove, but I'm anxious and awkward and I'm only inching back into my musical headspace.

I'm starting to groove when Jonathan stops the band again to pick something up. Ricky says, "Hey, Mark, you sound great, man."

"Thanks, brother." That helped.

There's silence in the room while Jonathan fumbles for whatever he's looking for. I feel flush and tortured inside. I kind of want to curl up on the floor.

It's a metronome. I see the red light blinking in perfect tempo, a jarring confirmation of my inadequacy. Jonathan tosses it to me underhand and mutters, "Watch the light." It's like tossing a calculator to an accountant. I sheepishly catch it and set it on the floor to my right side. I draw on every gram of energy to focus on that light. I look down and count off the band.

It's hard for me to harness my internal sense of time, let alone focus on a tiny light. I'm conflicted; my natural tendency is to look up while I'm playing, but the light pulls my focus back to the floor, stealing my energy from the very people I'm trying to engage. I feel like a scolded child.

When the song is done, I get the strong feeling that these rockers can't wait for me to leave. Jonathan says, "Well thanks a lot for coming out, Mark. Nice to meet ya." John and Neal give me dismissive nods and half-mast smiles. I grab my stick bag, relieved that it's over.

I walk out the door, and Ricky follows me. He says, "Hey man, you really sounded great. Thanks so much for coming. I'll stay in touch." He smiles and shakes my hand. I wipe off the sweat, thank him and walk down the corridor and out the door. I'm dizzy and exhausted.

In the car, I'm angry and frustrated. I sit there, replaying what I can remember. I'm defeated, my dreams of super group-dom destroyed, with no one to blame but myself. It was my moment to step up and through. And I didn't.

I go home and tell Michelle what happened. She consoles me. I'm blank. I play the audition over and over in my head for the rest of the day reconciling the defeat, analyzing my performance and exorcising the negative emotions.

Fortunately, I've never been one to wallow in self-pity. I wake up the next morning, feeling a bit invigorated and inspired, and I make two vows.

No. 1: I'll fortify my internal sense of meter so that no one can ever tell me again that I'm rushing or dragging unless I'm choosing to do so.

No. 2: I will break my nerves and fear into submission. I will learn how to harness that energy and those emotions and transform them into highly skilled, confident and powerful performances.

Move From Anxiety to Confidence

For the next year, I took on vow No. 1 and worked diligently with a metronome at nearly every tempo from 40 to 220 beats per minute, getting comfortable and confident playing multiple styles of music and and types of transitions. Vow No. 2 inspired me to begin the journey to build my confidence and harness my courage. I analyzed, studied, researched, networked and discovered until I uncovered the rituals and habits that now enable me to conquer fright, on and off the stage, and transform it into confidence.

These methods—which I fondly call the Three Cs—work. Since that audition, I've performed with some of the greatest musical artists in modern history: Beyoncé, Cher, Sheryl Crow, Foreigner, Al Green, Billy Idol, Dave Koz, Udo Lindenberg, Richard Marx, Stevie Nicks, The O'Jays, P!NK, Simple

Minds, Tina Turner, Velvet Revolver, Eikichi Yazawa and many others.

I've played the Grammy Awards—broadcast live across the globe to millions of people—three times. Heck, I played for 220,000 people at a single show in Glastonbury, England, with Simple Minds. There were so many people in that audience, it looked like rolling hills covered with people. It required three time-delayed sound systems synced to three video screens.

But I'm not the only performer here. We're all performers—like William Shakespeare wrote in *As You Like It*: "All the world's a stage, and all the men and women merely players." What I want to share with you is my experience, so that you'll have the inspiration, guts and tools to step up and through your defining moments when you're afraid or too intimidated to perform at your best, whether that be leading a meeting at work, presenting a sales pitch, giving a toast at your best friend's wedding, interviewing for a job, asking someone out on a date, resolving a family issue, closing a big deal, adding a campfire harmony to a classic rock song or giving a keynote to 5,000 people.

Merriam-Webster defines anxiety as an abnormal and overwhelming sense of apprehension and fear often marked by a) physiological signs (sweating, tension and increased pulse), b) doubt concerning the reality and nature of the threat and c) self-doubt about your capacity to cope with it.

For most of us, "performance anxiety" is synonymous with "action anxiety"—fear of doing something. This can impede our financial, social and even spiritual potential and goals. In fact, performance anxiety differs from other fears in that it affects not only cognition (thought) and physiology (body) but also behavior (action). For most people and in most circumstances, peak performance doesn't start with being calm. It comes from a balance between physical provocation or excitement and the brain's interpretation of this excitement.

According to Dr. Andrew Steptoe of University College London, "Performance improves with increasing arousal up to an intermediate level, but deteriorates as arousal rises beyond the optimum."[1]

Now, most people need a certain amount of nervousness or tension to perform at their best—as you will find evidenced in this book. So, let's say that "performance anxiety" is deleterious anxiety—the tipping point when physical manifestations become extreme and/or thought processes impede or distort. These physical effects may include heart palpitations and rapid heart rate, muscle weakness and tension, fatigue, nausea, chest pain, shortness of breath, headache, stomach ache or tension headaches.

---

[1] Dr. Andrew Steptoe, "Performance Anxiety. Recent Developments in Its Analysis and Management," *The Musical Times*, Vol. 123, No. 1674 (August 1982): 537-541.

Know Your Three Cs

In 2011, I came up with "Conquering Life's Stage Fright" as a topic for some of my speaking gigs. I'm passionate about the subject and love discussing it with others. Over the course of my life, I've performed for nearly a billion people. The resulting experiences and stories—combined with my methods of harnessing and moving through fear—have helped a lot of people. But I wanted to reach more.

My wife, Lisa, suggested I bring in other voices—ask top performers in all areas of life and business to share their stories of overcoming performance anxiety. That inspired me to interview more than 50 amazing people who have contributed potent stories and endorsements for my concepts.

Those interviews comprised my latest quest for insights and paralleled my 2011-2012 tour with Foreigner and my 2012 tour with P!NK. That journey introduced me to many talented, successful and confident people, and their inspiration, insight, stories and philosophies truly amplified my understanding of the Three Cs.

People were not only receptive to the interviews—they were excited about the concept. Interviewees included executives such as Zappos CEO Tony Hsieh (the passionate keynote) and Mark Papia, chief revenue officer of Connexity (the successful salesman); athletes such as Robbie Gould of the Chicago Bears (the lonely kicker) and Garrett McNamara (the experiential surfer); celebrities such as actor Jeremy Piven (the strategic performer) and Guy Fieri (the chef who cares); and, of course, musical artists such as Stewart Copeland of the Police (the beta-blocking drummer) and my buddy Dave Koz (the respectful saxophonist). Others don't fit any such categories—such as astronaut Alan Bean who walked on the moon and author/leadership coach Dr. Ronda Beaman who relies on "acting" confident.

There's a consistent, similar path that applies to how these top-class performers, presenters and communicators surpass anxiety and actualize their goals, and that path leads us sequentially through the Three Cs.

1. **Clarity.** Identify your goal and determine the skills you need to get there.
2. **Capability.** Become proficient in those skills.
3. **Confidence.** Success in your new skills naturally leads you to confidence.

Clarity is the first anxiety buster. I knew before I auditioned for Bad English that I lacked skill in some way—in that case, my ability to control internal sense of time. I wasn't prepared to be in a world-class band. My anxiety was appropriate; I was out of my league.

But it wasn't until I knew what I was missing that I could create the mindset to move forward. I'll show you how to establish clarity relative to your level of knowledge and performance early on, which will enable you to cut through distractions and ambiguity and define your true goal. The moment you clarify that true goal, and where you stand relative to it, you'll know what you need to do. There's no mystery, and that diffuses the anxiety.

Capability represents preparation, education, the proper feeding of the mind and the appropriate execution of skills. You're busting through barriers and solving problems to achieve the goal that you clarified. I lacked some real fundamentals in the area of meter. The way to develop those fundamentals was to get busy working with a metronome (the very symbol of my failure).

If you're capable, you're accomplished, talented, proficient, skilled and able to do a particular thing well. When you're prepared, you're at your highest level of performance or presentation. This is paramount to fundamentally reducing fear; you have no question about the capability you have worked hard and smart to create. Always ask yourself if you can really do what you claim. If you're just puffing, then it's time to rewind and continue developing your capability.

Confidence is the state of being certain. It's the simple and powerful result of clarifying your goal and becoming capable. I'm now completely confident in my ability to control my internal sense of meter.

For example: While writing this, I've just started rehearsing with P!NK for her world tour. We're playing some of the songs I've played hundreds of times on the last two tours. But on Day 1, I got a refreshing hint of nervousness when we broke into "Just Like a Pill" and "So What." But I was energized and confident, because I knew I was prepared.

I have clarity, capability and, therefore, total confidence in my goal—performing these songs. I'm clear about what I have to do to play the new songs, and as I play them more and more, I'll develop capability and eventually be totally confident with them.

Keep in mind the power of the three Cs once you've gained confidence. They're more than just the process toward setting goals; they can also be applied to small steps long after you've gained confidence. If an upcoming presentation or performance is bringing you anxiety that you think could impede peak performance—even after you think you've worked the three Cs and even successfully presented—then it's time to take a step back and clarify what you may be missing.

- Is there a new piece of information that you need to incorporate?
- Have circumstances changed or is there some new component or person you need to address?
- Have you learned something that you still need to flesh out in your presentation?

The three Cs are potent and applicable to all stages of learning and development.

I've also included action items you can do as you move through these three steps. My recent journey visiting with performers, professionals, athletes and speakers has reiterated their value. As you read, you'll become acquainted with some of the most successful people on the planet and their sensational stories. These stories will inspire you as you become clear, capable and confident.

In The 7 Habits of Highly Successful People, Stephen R. Covey asks his readers to keep the goal of teaching the concepts to others in mind. He suggests that when you read something with the intention of communicating it out, you pay special attention to the details of the content. I invite you to do the same.

I started this journey two decades ago, but it's not just mine anymore. It belongs to you; it belongs to the world. Time to get started. Rock on!

SECTION 1: CLARITY

"Champions do not become champions when they win the event, but in the hours, weeks, months and years they spend preparing for it. The victorious performance itself is merely the demonstration of their championship character." —Alan Armstrong, author

Your ultimate goal is to confidently take action—to perform to your fullest capability—and the best first step is to clarify how much you actually know.

Use these four levels of competence (adapted from Abraham Maslow's hierarchy of needs) to define where you stand. Remember, when you remove the mystery, you reduce the fear and anxiety, and your path to confidence becomes clear. Understanding these levels and how they relate to the three Cs will make your road easier.

1. Unconscious Incompetence (clarity). You don't know what you don't know. What a relaxed and easy place to be! There's a reason "ignorance is bliss" is cliché—until that naïveté hits us in the face or crushes our hearts and egos. I didn't know that my tempo was that inconsistent before the Bad English audition. And when I found out, it was painful...and totally enlightening. That's when I entered the most exhilarating (and difficult) level of learning.

2. Conscious Incompetence (clarity). You recognize what it is that you don't know or what you can't do. You acknowledge the value in it as well. Making mistakes can be integral to the learning process at this stage. For me, this was the point when I realized the power that developing my meter would give me.

3. Conscious Competence (capability). You can do it. You can ride the bike, do the math, make the speech—even play consistently in time with a metronome. But you still have to concentrate really hard, because you haven't mastered the skill yet. After a year or so of conscious incompetence, I realized my ability to (at least more easily) play tempos, weave in and out of drum fills between beats and even change styles from rock to funk to jazz to Latin—all while playing right with the metronome. And, I eventually found a new realm of comfort playing without it.

4. Mastery (confidence). You're there. If you get behind the wheel, start up the car and drive to work with little conscious thought about the mechanics of your driving, you've mastered driving. My accountant, Mark, uses his calculator at lightning speed without even looking at it. I've become so comfortable playing with a metronome that I can play with it, behind it, ahead of it and even start and stop it during my performances (which I do sometimes just to check the tempo of the band). While I'm playing, I'm not giving my tempo conscious thought. I'm highly competent. I'm comfortable teaching this skill and have a how-to-work-with-a-metronome section in my instructional DVD.

GAIN CLARITY

Questions

1. What do I want to be good (or better) at?
2. On a scale of 0 to 10, what is my competence level?
3. How do I know this?
4. What are the skills I need to master to become confident?
5. What do I need to learn to be able to demonstrate this mastery?
6. From whom or where can I learn these skills?
7. How much practice and time will it take for me to master them?

Mission

Create a six-month plan for raising your skill level, and detail how you will rate your success.

Chapter 1: Define the Why

Garrett McNamara holds the record for largest wave ever surfed and he has a simple and important belief about clarifying goals: Make sure you're doing it for the right reasons. "If you're doing anything for quick satisfaction, because there's a camera on the cliff or there's big prize money, you're going out for the wrong reasons and you're doing it for ego," he says.

When I think about what the "why" behind my Bad English audition, I realize that I was actually driven by a passionate fantasy that I'd had since I was a kid—to be a rock star. When I made those two vows afterward, I zeroed in on my true purpose—to master my instrument—and I actually developed a deeper passion for my purpose. This motivated me to really want to do the work to become truly capable. My path and my skill set needed to be clear, and I didn't have either one before or during the audition. Any drum teacher would have told me to focus on those capabilities, and get the stars out of my eyes.

It's like author James Allen, a pioneer of the self-help movement, wrote, "They who have no central purpose in their life fall an easy prey to petty worries."[2]

Passion gets you interested in something—particularly for artists—but purpose makes you identify it (clarity) and get to work (capability). Understanding why you do something can motivate you further. If you want to control your mind and the negative byproducts of your thoughts, keep it busy and focused with a purpose.

When you define your purpose, you become passionate about it, and that can be the deepest passion you ever know. When I visited the Zappos office in Las Vegas, I was astonished by the passion there. Everyone I met oozed passion and pride in an almost fairytale business environment. Every area has a theme. Every desk (and many ceilings) represents its owner's personality. Street signs hang above cubicle rows to help employees and visitors identify where they are on campus. The walls are graffitied with personal mantras, quotes, accomplishments and signatures. The energy was more pep rally than workplace.

After reading CEO Tony Hsieh's book, *Delivering Happiness: A Path to*

---

[2] James Allen, *As a Man Thinketh* (New York: Jeremy P. Tarcher, 2008), 27.

Profits, Passion, and Purpose, I realized that each employee at Zappos was carefully selected because of his or her understanding and desire to operate with a deep and unified purpose. Everyone I spoke with had complete clarity about living the company's core values (such as "create fun and a little weirdness" and "deliver WOW through service").

Tony says, "If you're passionate about something, and you know it inside and out, then it's way easier. Rather than memorizing a speech you've written, just talk about stuff that you're passionate about and that you already know. Then, all you really need are the high-level bullet points, and it's just like a conversation with anyone."

It doesn't feel like work. When you remind yourself of the reason why you chose to do your presentation, performance, launch or meeting, you can cultivate that passion. Tap into that purpose when you feel anxious.

Chicago Bears kicker Robbie Gould confirmed for me the power of intense focus on goal, and how clarity quells anxiety. "You've got to make every kick. That's the mentality. The mentality is you're only as good as your last kick. My mentality is that I'm only as good as my next kick—because I can't do anything about what happened in the past. I can only learn from that and make it better for myself and for my team going forward."

Robbie's also very clear about why he's doing his job.

"I want the ball for the last-second field goal to win or lose the game. I want to be that guy who everyone knows they can rely on in those situations. And, at the end of the day, if you don't think that you're going to be the best, or strive to be the best, at that position, then your career is probably gonna be a lot shorter.

"I don't know how many kickers are gonna make it into the hall of fame. But I hope I have a hall-of-fame-type career. If you're not striving to be the best in your league, or the best guitarist, the best drummer, the best linebacker, the best quarterback, you're probably going to be just another guy, and you're not going to make the biggest impact on your team or in the community. When I say I'm going to do something, I'm all in, and I'm going to dedicate everything I have to doing it, and if that's not good enough, then at the end of the day it just wasn't meant to be."

ACTION STEP:
GAIN CLARITY

Mission

Recall a time when you had clarity about your purpose and felt empowered and passionate. Recall as much detail about that moment as you can—where you were, the time of day, the environment, who you were with, the smell, the temperature, what you were wearing—to really bring you back to that moment. If you could have seen the future, what positive feelings would you have?

Chapter 2: Prepare, Prepare, Prepare

Clarity can be enlightening (you discover ideas, concepts, skills and opportunities that you didn't know existed) or painful (you face what you don't know and what you can't do) depending on when you become aware of your nescience and how you see it. With clarity, you become aware of what you don't know, and it's easy to retreat in the face of incompetence and fall back into unconscious bliss (but you're reading this book, so you have a thirst for knowledge and desire to remain conscious).

That Bad English audition, and the knowledge it brought, crushed me... for a day. After that I swore that my internal sense of meter (and its faults), would never again thwart my career. I knew what I needed to do. After researching teachers and courses, I enrolled in a rhythm class and spent the next few years married to a metronome. It was a clear goal, and I became very capable.

Erik Weihenmayer, the first blind person to top Mount Everest, sees fear as an enemy...and a friend. "Sometimes fear tells you that you're truly not ready for something, that you need to prepare more, that you need to train more or that you need to get more comfortable in a crazy environment."

I got chills when Erik talked about going through Everest's Khumbu Icefall. "You don't cross through it once. You cross through it 10 times to acclimatize. You're setting yourself up for your higher camps, and you're getting your body used to breathing less and less oxygen. It's a physiological preparation. You have to increase the hemoglobin, your body's ability to absorb more oxygen. So, you cross through the icefall and climb the mountain, up and down and up and down to train your body and your cells to breathe in more oxygen."

One key component to clarity is becoming aware of contingencies. Erik talks a lot about the mind-body connection. He told himself that he was committed; he was going through the icefall no matter what. He took deep breaths and stilled his mind. All the thoughts rushing through his brain would only hurt him at "go time." Once he reached the icefall, he'd been through dozens of "don't fall" moments—he'd been preparing for three years.

Erik's currently learning the ins and outs of whitewater kayaking, and he remembers navigating the Usumacinta River in Southeast Mexico last winter.

"It's massive, and there are whirlpools that swirl across the entire width of the river, six feet deeper than the surface of the water. They grab your kayak, and they suck you down and flip you sometimes—especially if you can't see. So, you're upside down getting violently spun around. You're trying to roll up in an Eskimo roll, and it's really, really scary.

"I came home from that river with something like post-traumatic stress disorder. I got in over my head several times, and I was totally in panic and survival mode. I realized that that wasn't necessarily good for my training; it totally shattered my confidence. So, I had to go back to a place where I was comfortable, almost starting over, and go through some rapids that I could get through."

It was critical for Erik to clearly define his skill level. "I took five steps back, and it worked. I rewired my brain enough that I have confidence now, and I'm back doing a little bit bigger stuff. It's a tricky thing all the time. It's not always like, 'Just go for it,' because life can kill ya in the mountains."

My ex-wife, Kelly Gallagher, a producer and writer, has tackled mountains of her own. She has gone to war against cancer five different times and won each battle. Her triumphs include 86 blood transfusions, three pacemakers, multiple chemotherapy and radiation treatments. Imagine the profound anxiety of facing your first stem-cell transplant. Kelly went up against some unbelievable odds, and has not only survived but also thrived.

How? She had clarity. One of the keys to her survival was the empowerment she gained as an active participant in her healing, and she refused to give up that control to the doctor(s) administering the cure(s). That never made sense to Kelly. She was constantly on quests for the information and engagement that could give her better odds at winning the war. It took a lot of preparation.

"I was an extreme athlete once upon a time. No pain, no gain, physically and mentally. Cancer was the ultimate distance event. It required such clear focus: count my vitamins, count my food, do the (coffee) enema…did I lay in the ozone body bag?"

It also became clear to her that not everyone would completely and totally comprehend her process —not her bosses, not her friends. "When you're supposed to be at an event, and you're late, people don't really understand. 'Why can't you get there? Why isn't she doing this?' It's the focus.

"My swim coach intimidated me into preparation. I'm swimming in the same lane as the girl who has world records in the 1,500-meter freestyle and the 500-meter freestyle. He says, 'If she laps you, then you'll swim butterfly the rest of your life!' I tactically knew how to beat her—if she had a false start, and I won by default. That was the only way I could ever beat this girl. It was clear. When it came time for cancer, I couldn't afford to be in second place."

She needed to be very clear about her plan, and part of that plan involved taking the risks she credits for her survival. "I listened to outliers and alternative medicine renegades who were far from mainstream. That's a risk some people are not willing to take. My lack of supervision in my cancer therapies saved my life. And there was really nobody to tell me, 'No.'"

Kelly also built an international support system to keep her in the mix and on the cutting edge of information and technology when it came to adjunct therapies. She calls the team her pit crew. "I ran things fast, and I opened up my case to a team of doctors on the Internet that chimed in from China, Germany, Seattle and Dallas. My friend Tom Clabor runs that think tank, and there are a lot of people who comment. He has a science experiment every time something is going on. I have a preparedness team, and I'm clear about what to do."

Chapter 3: Get to the Finish Line

Most people don't spend enough time on clarity. I know I didn't, even as a professional drummer. When I got my butt handed to me at that Bad English audition, I knew it was time to clarify. That clarity allowed me to become more capable, which led to a natural growth of confidence, and there you have it!

When I started on this book, I found myself running down a rabbit hole—the more I researched, the more I wanted to include and the more confused I became.

I started experiencing some serious anxiety. So, I called my dear friend, Jim Samuels, who's been my teacher and mentor for more than 25 years. Some of his unique philosophies are in this book. He told me to narrow my goal to one sentence with three defining points. In other words, he asked me to clarify.

My goal: I want my book to be well ordered, potent and entertaining. Every word, sentence and paragraph needed to reflect this goal. Whatever did not, I needed to lose. With this clarity, my path was defined, and the anxiety subsided.

Without clarity, there's no way to succeed, because there's no finish line. How would you even know if you crossed it? Clarity covers a lot, not only as a starting point, but also as a finishing point. Pinpointing your goal keeps you focused. It's your mission statement. It's your mantra—the simpler, the better.

ACTION STEP:
CLARIFY YOUR GOAL

What is your goal? Is it to a) provide information or explain an idea, b) persuade your audience to see things your way or c) move people to action?

Chapter 4: Hone Your Human GPS

I've researched how people define GPS as it relates to the human condition, and I think Jim Samuels' philosophy is the simplest and most effective. His formula: Goal, problem, solution. We set goals, and then solve problems that arise as a result of those goals. If you're thirsty, you get a glass of water. It's actually quite sophisticated, but you handle it unconsciously.

Now, most of us, at one point or another, will create a negative goal. I did it during the Bad English audition. I needed to focus on rock solid, steady meter, but my "don't rush, Mark, don't rush" moved me in the wrong direction. That brain is a mindful child and tends to cooperate with what we emphasize, especially when we're under duress or our sensibilities are impeded by anxiety. In those moments, a negative goal will never give you the clarity to be capable.

In that situation, your true goal is obscured. Without clarity, you end up solving the wrong problems and finding solutions that actually distract you from what you really want.

People spend a lot of time solving problems that obscure goals and create busy work. Stop trying to work through unnecessary challenges, and figure out the path to your goals. Does that involve problem solving? Yes, but always ask yourself if the task at hand or the problem you encounter is leading you back to your goal. If it isn't, you need to stop doing or trying to solve it.

First, define the length of your goal—short-, mid- or long-term. This will help you clarify your path and build confidence. Every time you accomplish a goal, no matter how big or small, you create a win for yourself. As you accumulate more wins, your confidence grows—the ratio of confidence-to-fear tips more and more in your favor.

You are also solidifying your integrity. Like transformational models expert Werner Erhard wrote, "By keeping your word, we mean doing what you said you would do and by the time you said you would do it."[3]

There is much power in taking action, specifically the exact action you agree to do. This agreement can be with yourself or others. Remember that the end goal isn't to reduce your anxiety but to build confidence.

My short-term goal was picking a tempo or tempo range for each practice

---

[3] Werner Erhard, Michael C. Jensen and Steve Zaffron, "Integrity: A Positive Model that Incorporates the Normative Phenomena of Morality, Ethics and Legality," http://papers.ssrn.com/sol3/papers.cfm?abstract_id=1542759 (March 2009).

session and getting to the point where I could clap along with a metronome for a minute and not hear it click. I needed to get so synchronized with the metronome that my clapping and that metronome beep were one. It required stopping and starting many times until I found complete concentration. Depending on my concentration and daily skill set, this could take 10 minutes or more than three hours, but eventually I could "bury the click" at tempo ranges from 40 to 220 beats per minute.

My mid-range goal was to play my drum set for a minute to the same tempo range, moving in and out of basic beats, fills, style changes and transitions, while cancelling that click the entire time.

Long-term, I wanted to master playing with the click. I can now play all tempos and all styles, moving in and out of fills and transitions and burying that click for an entire song. I can do this in any situation—the recording studio, live shows or seminars—in front of anyone. I can also play behind the click or ahead of the click. This has come in handy when the click is slightly out of sync from the rest of the recorded track, which happens in the recording studio when a producer wants a track where the click is a bit delayed. In live rehearsals with P!NK, we often receive tracks from the record, and when we play with them the first few times, the clicks are slightly ahead or behind the music. I'm ready; I can shift the placement of my drumming to accommodate.

ACTION STEP:
HONE YOUR GPS

Mission
1. Write down something you want.
2. List the problems standing between you and achieving your goal.
3. Focus on each problem until you come up with a solution that moves you closer to fulfilling that goal.
4. What is your short-term or daily goal?
5. What is your mid-term, weekly or monthly goal?
6. What is your long-term or life goal?

Chapter 5: Make the Audience Your Drug of Choice

Now, clarity has great value beyond goal-setting. You need clarity when considering your audience, and its needs, wants and desires. That clarity gives you a double edge. The more detailed intel you have about your audience, the more they will feel like you know them, whether they are clients, employees, family members or fans. You build your own confidence, and the confidence your audiences have in you, because you have a good idea about their desires, pains and aspirations.

Dr. Solomon Hamburg, a doctor of oncology at Cedars-Sinai Medical Center, says people should never be ashamed when they communicate or present. I value his opinion; he's one of the foremost communicators and speakers in the medical industry. "A lot of anxieties for me come from worrying about being judged. If you get away from outside judgment, you're more confident with yourself."

As a child, Dr. Sol had a severe stutter. He could read perfectly out loud in an empty room; his anxiety came from the projection that people were judging him. So, he spent a lot of time gaining clarity, doing exercises and telling himself not to worry about potential critics.

One tip: Dr. Sol says your audience probably won't remember the exact details of what you say, anyhow.

"You really don't come away with everything a person said—you come away with a feeling. When I listen to someone play the drums, I don't remember how many times you hit the cymbal. I remember the gestalt, the big picture. People tell themselves that everybody is watching their every move or listening to their every word; we don't really look at people like that. When you see a good-looking woman, you don't look just at her nose or her eyes, it's the whole picture. With audiences, they're judging the big picture. That's critical to helping calm me down."

Dr. Sol pays more attention to his audience's ability to understand him, in a convention hall or in his office. As a kid, in moments of true selflessness, his stuttering would stop, like when he translated his mother's Yiddish at the butcher store. The experience also helped him develop an appreciation for the art of simplification—a form of clarity. It's an audience-centric approach to communicating, especially when it's easy to become overly technical—and potentially lose attention.

"I had to simplify things. English words don't necessarily translate into Yiddish easily, and vice versa. So, let's say a piece of steak has a lot of gristle in it. But, I can't use the word 'gristle.' There's no word for 'gristle' in Yiddish. I have to use the word 'fat.' Now, I'm used to translating jargon into common language." If there are patients who don't like the fact that I simplify things, I send them to Dr. Fred Rosenthal who's very stodgy and formal."

Most people feel more comfortable performing in front of lots of people than in front of a couple. Zappos CEO Tony Hsieh says his ideal audience is at least 500 people. The audience size he hates the most: 50. It's too big for him to make a connection with each person, but too small for his jokes to really go over. He says bigger crowds make everything seem funnier. And eye contact? "I've read books that suggest that you find three people and make eye contact with each person. I don't do that. That doesn't work for me."

It's smart to clarify the method that does work best for you. P!NK makes eye contact with as many people as possible, and she talks to an audience of 20,000 as if it's in her living room. When we hang out one-on-one, she talks to me the same way.

Entrepreneur and CEO David Kalt perspires when he gets passionate about something. He says the condition was particularly bad when he was holding investor meetings prior to the stock market launch of his Chicago Music Exchange. To stem the tide, he used eye contact.

"If I could make eye contact and play offense, I'd feel much more comfortable than being on defense. That wasn't very natural to me, because I'm more of a laid back, relaxed kind of guy. I'm not very aggressive. I'm not super-competitive. But in the context of a business meeting, there are two, three or four people, and you immediately have the opportunity to set the stage and get in a position where you feel strength and confidence," David explained. "I realized I had to actually make eye contact and make that visual connection—and then it all just came up from there.

"I use my eyes because people have told me in the past that when I get excited, there's a glitter in my eye. When people tell you that, you've got to figure out how to use it. So, I figured out how to use that eye technique to immediately dazzle and deliver. Then, it just came out as confidence, because I felt like I had a little bit of an edge in the room. Anybody who is passionate about something has that gleam in his or her eyes. Everybody's got it, this passion. There's something about the body that physically changes, and the eyes always sparkle if you're truly, authentically passionate about something."

Mark Papia, chief revenue officer for Connexity, has a powerful tool for addressing a big audience. "When you're speaking in front of a group of 20 people or a group of 2,000 people, you deal with that by not focusing on the fact that there are 2,000 people looking at you, you deal with that by thinking about the fact that it's you and an audience. It's one of you and one of them."

But some meetings are still just plain nerve-wracking. "I've gone to meetings where you go out in the startup world and you raise money. When you have those types of meetings, there might be 20 people in the room. So, it's a big enough number that it's a little jolting, but it's not so big that it's completely unnerving.

"It would blow your mind how many presenters don't take the time to introduce themselves to the audience individually. Everybody says, 'Thanks for coming today. I'm excited to be here. I represent Connexity and we're looking to do a Series B, and I'm going to lay out our value.' You'd be shocked to learn how few people stand at the door and introduce themselves to people as they walk in or take the time away from the presentation to introduce themselves and shake hands."

But there's going to be a point in the presentation when you're going to ask if anybody has a question, Mark says. And what typically happens? Either nobody wants to be the first to raise a hand or nobody cared enough about your presentation to actually want to go one step further. And you can get that 60 seconds of awkwardness when you're looking around the room begging for somebody to just raise a hand.

"I always introduce myself," he says. "That breaks the ice with every one of those 20 people. And when you say, 'Hey, does anybody have any questions?' All of a sudden, there are three or four hands up. Those questions tend to be an important compliment to your presentation."

You're actually creating a deeper level of connectivity, and you're gaining clarity with your audience. People are going to communicate with you on a personal level because they've actually met you. I've used a similar tactic during some of my seminars when the audience numbers less than 100. When I get introduced, I go right into the audience and shake everyone's hand while laughing and creating a comfortable and personal environment.

Then I say, "This feels like we are all friends hanging out, so feel free to raise your hands at any point during my presentation and ask any question you like."

Questions

1. Do they know me personally?
2. Do they have prejudices about me? Do I have prejudices about them?
3. What are our similarities and potential shared experiences? Our differences?
4. Are there any barriers in communication for which I can prepare?
5. Are they knowledgeable about my topic?
6. How much background do they need, if any?
7. How much can they relate to my topic?
8. How will my planned presentation give the audience what they need?
9. What else can I do to maximize their takeaway value?
10. Is there still anything I may be missing to make their experiences better?

Regardless of audience size, I'm happier, more effective and vastly more generous when I turn my attention away from myself, and gain that clarity around my audience.

Last year, I performed at a tribute to the late, great Led Zeppelin drummer John Bonham. This was not only a performance for fans; there were 21 of the most accomplished drummers on the planet performing in the same show. I wasn't really overwhelmed with nervousness, but some self-imposed things got in the way of me really enjoying the journey.

After my performance, I was disappointed and embarrassed—I didn't think I played well. Even after some heartfelt endorsements from friends, my viewpoint remained rigid. And my attitude was not only undermining my ability to enjoy the rest of the show, but it was impeding my sense of judgment and sanity. I wasn't nearly as present and supportive of my peers as I would have been with a clear head, and I just beat myself up more as the night went on, comparing myself to the other drummers rather than enjoying the wonderful opportunity.

I got a chance to play again in the finale, as we all took turns playing solos to Zeppelin's "Moby Dick," and my thoughts were so distorted by that point

I couldn't turn things around to feel as though I was playing anywhere near my best.

I lost nearly a full night's sleep to self-loathing, and that's not how I usually operate. It wasn't until my manager, Stephen Stern, sent me a YouTube link and I watched the performance that I realized I'd actually played pretty darn well. The experience galvanized my belief that it's not about me. It's about integrating with my audience and having a healthy and accurate sense of self rather than a potentially unhealthy fixation on self.

I've played with the band Foreigner intermittently since 1992, but the most recent tour gave me more joy than just about any other gig. When I was playing with the band circa 1994, I had a very different experience.

We'd been on the road for nearly 18 months, and I was burned out. One night after a show, I realized that I'd (ironically) played "Feels Like the First Time" more than 300 times—and I just wasn't feeling all that excited about it. In fact, it was kind of mundane. And that was really selfish. The show wasn't for me; it was for the audience. At that moment, I wanted a little stage fright, just to feel the emotion.

My clarity: I needed to focus on them—those screaming, happy fans, and their joy and excitement. I started thinking about my first rock concerts: Peter Frampton, Boston and, yes, Foreigner. (I'm not an original member; I saw this band when I was a teenager.) And something really weird happened; I got a hint of butterflies.

What the hell had I been doing? How selfish I'd been! So shameful and self-absorbed, I forgot the reason I was playing. The next day, I went onstage before the show and drew a big, ridiculous, happy face with large teeth on the head of my snare drum as a reminder to be audience-centric and selfless onstage. And every night for the rest of the tour, I got on stage, grinned at that face (which I re-drew every time my tech, Paulie, changed the head), found a bunch of gratitude and connected with my audience.

Celebrity chef Guy Fieri once asked orator Zig Ziglar how to get rid of the butterflies. His answer? "The day that that happens will be the day you don't do as well." You need that little bit of fear to remind you to respect those moments and the consequences, or you start getting sloppy. "That's true," Guy says. "It's something that I've lived by my whole career."

Guy gets nervous because he cares. He takes on the responsibility of performing well, because his audiences or customers deserve the full value of their money.

Selfishness can kill or exaggerate stage fright at will. But the risk is worth it. No matter if I'm performing, auditioning, interviewing or playing with my daughter—it's not about me. So, when I start to get too nervous, I now think, "You selfish bastard! It's not about you!" This makes me laugh and squelches the nerves.

Just remember, people don't love you because you're perfect. I learned that from my friend Dr. Paul Stoltz, author of *Adversity Quotient*. He frequently serves as a source for the world's top media (CNN, CNBC, PBS). He notes that people actually love you for your imperfections, and how you handle those. "Why was TV detective Columbo so endearing? Because he was a fumbling, bumbling, faltering, brilliant guy."

Paul remembers his first gig for a multinational insurance company at its corporate retreat in a remote village outside Johannesburg. Electrical connectivity was dicey for a presentation that was wholly driven off his laptop. There were adapters and power strips everywhere. The crowd seemed very unforgiving. But he took a breath and laid into it: "Today, we need to talk about the thing that none of you are strangers to. Today, we're gonna talk about adversity."

And the audience started to laugh. "I thought that was the weirdest reaction. Did I say it wrong? Are they thinking I have no cred? Then, this guy pointed behind me, and there was smoke rising off the keyboard on my laptop." The audience started clapping; it was brilliant. And Paul realized the opportunity at hand and went with it.

His advice: Gain clarity before your big presentation or sales pitch. "Be connected, authentic, effective and impactful. The biggest shift for me was when I got outside my own skin and stopped having it be about me and made it about being obsessed with them. Then, by definition, you're not nervous, because you're scanning, looking, responding and adjusting, real time, all the time. And that changes the whole gig."

That's when you stop listening to the voice in your head that second-guesses your work, the one that screams, "That gesture didn't work. You have to move faster. Talk more." Paul knows that voice starts to vaporize when you become infatuated with your audience. People know when that's real.

He says the biggest trap in presenting is ego.

"The worst and biggest compliment for me was when I was a young, precocious buck—people kept telling me what a great and skilled presenter I was. Now, I think that's a slap and an insult, because that means they're paying attention to something in my technique of presenting. That's getting in the way of what I'm trying to say. The message has to conquer the mode of delivery. Now, when someone says that, I'm disappointed. I really am. I'm almost morose. They thought I was putting on a show. They were more focused on my methodology of delivering than my message."

He reminds me of Dr. Zubin Damania, or ZDoggMD. Their performances are completely different, but their techniques are similar. ZDogg also has clarity of goal—to be audience-centric. He's a board-certified internist and clinical hospitalist and now lives in downtown Las Vegas performing medical satire. He says that ego is detrimental to quality performance. It gets in the way of connecting with the audience, and that builds antagonism.

"You can't make the audience your enemy. 'I feel like these guys just don't get my jokes. They're not getting what I'm saying. What's wrong with these guys?' That's your defense mechanism," he says. "You've read them wrong. That isn't the way they learn, and it's not the way they're geared."

When you read the audience and empathize with it, you change lives. In *Give Your Speech, Change the World*, Nick Morgan explains that every presentation is an opportunity to move your audience to action. Be selfless, audience-centric and allow extraordinary things to happen for you and them—that's the most rewarding reason to do a performance anyway.

ZDogg thinks performing is a privilege, and I agree. He recalls a speech—15 minutes of stand-up comedy—he performed for 1,300 ER doctors in San Francisco. Afterward, several military physician assistants approached him and said, "We're some of the least happy people because of how we're treated, our workload and what we see. Just listening to you for 15 minutes gave us a new perspective—we all go through this sort of thing, and we have to keep our core identities. Thank you."

And that's what ZDogg aims for every time. Being audience-centric reminds us of the very reason we're performing or presenting—providing music, information or just a great experience. It helps us turn our energy outward. Return to your goal, and the audience will direct your energy back to success.

There are differences in what propels people to higher states of confidence. It's noteworthy that some people do better with a smooth, well-planned presentation and some thrive on the spontaneous actions or challenges from the audience. You just need clarity on which is best for you.

I'm currently putting together a new presentation based on the concepts in this book. Some of my best (and worst) moments have occurred because of technical blunders with equipment during presentations. Now, I often purposefully incorporate some snafu into my presentation, only to resolve it and let the audience witness the process. How you deal with mistakes, the way you compensate, utilize and invite adversity can give you clarity and freedom that set you free from fear of the unplanned.

Marc Cenedella, founder and executive chairman of TheLadders.com, likes a challenge to build his confidence. "Having grown up in a family of four boys, I actually perform better if somebody's asking me tough questions or getting into a little bit of a fight with me. Because that kind of stiffens my spine, and I get more excited about the fight than I do about worrying whether I'm doing well."

Early in his career, my saxophonist buddy Dave Koz analyzed how viewers responded to entertainers while he was in the audience. He came to some distinct conclusions. "You have to be sensitive. People who are great in real life—not just in music, but also in life—are sensitive to their surroundings. They can read a room. They understand. They don't barge in and say, 'I'm here now, and whatever is important to me is going to be.' The great ones walk into a room. They scan it, they read it, they feel it and then they tinker with their message to deliver whatever they're receiving. They deliver a message that can be heard."

Being altruistic not only connects you with your audience, but with your fellow performers. Actor Jeremy Piven's mother, Joyce (a noted director, actress and theater instructor), tells her students to focus on their fellow actors (or the audience), not on themselves.

"The anxiety subsides once you launch into the belly of the beast, once you start playing and put the focus on the other players and not yourself," Jeremy says. "Then, you're on to something."

I tell my students to be the member of the band who listens, the one who's cool, and the one who's there for everyone else. That's the one who will go on to great things.

I now have a ritual before my performances: I close my eyes and focus my energy on inspiration, freedom, release and total sync with people. I put it out into the universe that some extraordinary, spontaneous and unexpected things will happen to enhance my performance, that everyone in the room will get the most out of the experience and that their lives and mine will be forever enhanced as a result.

This kind of clarity is universal. Take German superstar rocker Udo Lindenberg. He's better known in German-speaking territories than the chancellor. (He's now in his mid-60s, and his musical career is at its peak. He's also an accomplished painter, using colored liqueurs for his palette.) And he's made a career fighting xenophobia in his home country—Udo may well have influenced the razing of the Berlin Wall. His altruism led to his arrest on Red Square and an interrogation in a Moscow jail for bringing "panic and chaos" to the youths of the U.S.S.R. in the mid-1980s. He has received death threats: "This is going to be your last day. Gonna be your last 'Hallelujah, Amen.'" He's worn bulletproof jackets onstage—all because the audience is the most important thing to him.

Udo has always wanted to move and motivate people with his words. "I am a friend to them," he says. "It is a bridge that we build with the songs, because people know the songs since…forever. They were part of their lives, and part of their biographies. They love it, and they celebrate it. They are the friends who I have not seen yet, but know that they are. It's a big family. It's like having a big family meeting."

Even mixed martial artists get this. For Kendall Grove, a successful performance isn't about him; it's about his team. "These people invested more than just friendship. They invested time and energy teaching me. You don't want to let these people down. It's an individual sport, but you got to hold it down. You've got to think not just about yourself, but also about your crew, the people who've helped you. When I win, they win. When I lose, they lose."

NFL sideline reporter Laura Okmin remembers a specific time when she had to remain focused and clear on her goal—an interview with former NFL cornerback Michael Lehan, who was reticent of talking about his life in foster homes. In the course of her story package, Michael visited with some foster children. An 8-year-old boy, who had been molested by his father and uncle, raised his hand: "Can you tell me why bad things happen to good kids?"

"Sitting down with Michael afterward and having that conversation—he's crying. I literally sat there and pinched my leg because I wanted to lose it so badly," Laura says. "It was so emotional, and he was having one of those moments that I wanted to help him through and couldn't, and all I kept thinking in my head—I broke my rule, I never have an inner dialogue during an interview because then I'm not listening to what the person says—'It's not about you. It's not about you. It's not about you. If I start to cry now, we can't use my camera. And his reaction is going to change.'"

Prodigal Sunn of the Wu-Tang Clan focuses on the audience, too. He makes the stage his living room (just like P!NK). "I make everybody feel at home—the bartender, the bouncer, the security, the sound man, whoever's in the house. They all get love. You might even catch me in the crowd. You might catch me hangin' out front."

He recognizes people as people. You build up fear because you're worried about people's opinions; it stops you from performing at your best. "I started to feel this way recently, worrying about how I could reach out or become a brand. Just breathe. I remind myself that I'm here to be me and not my ego."

Prodigal goes all out for his audiences, sometimes above and beyond what his band wants to do. "Wu-Tang was invited to do a concert in Miami. And some of the group didn't wanna participate. But, me and the DJ had a connection. I went out there and did the show myself, even though the crowd wanted to see the group. I was confident enough in myself to know that I could hold it down. When I was out there, I got the respect of just being the guy who will show up. The crowd met me halfway. That takes the fear away, and that just grew me stronger."

He could have worried about what the crowd was expecting. Instead, he made it his goal to give the crowd the best experience he could.

"The universe and life are here to support you if you just do your part. At the end of the day, if it wasn't meant to be, it wouldn't have happened, just more of the things that you learn that make you stronger. I was there, and I still was having my ears and my eyes open, so I learned a lot.

The Wu-Tang Clan has been around for more than 20 years, but everything is still brand new to Prodigal.

"I've learned that what the ego conceives is sometimes a trap. At the end of the day, man, love what you do. Be who you are. Thoroughly enjoy your talents and your gifts, 'cause your spirit lays it out on you; you're that vessel. The ego will always pretend that it's together, even when it's not."

Mission

Think about a past performance or presentation that made you anxious. Was your attention focused on your anxiety or on your audience? Relive that event, this time focusing your attention completely on your audience. How does the experience change?

Chapter 6: Visualize

Lucy Streeter stared down 120 feet and 9 inches to the water below from her square-foot perch. And jumped. The speed as she descended clocked in at nearly 80 miles per hour. She claims to have had no fear, that she's "tough as nails."

She's jumped from the cliffs of Acapulco, where divers have to clear 22 feet and wait for a wave or be de-brained by the rocks below, but says, "I can't tell you really that I've ever been afraid. It's freedom to me. It's flying through the air, and I feel like I'm a bird. I just love speed, and I love the wind in my face."

Before I go out, I see myself doing the flip and landing perfectly straight up and down and squeezing as tight as I possibly can—because your body can be ripped apart as soon as you hit the water. I see myself coming up and waving and smiling to the crowd, ripping my entry. That's always huge. No splash when you go in. Just fffffewt. You know, poof! You're gone."

Her process of clarifying employs visualization, the process of using your imagination to create mental images. Creative visualization is a method people use to find success by imagining specific behaviors or events. It's the foundation for positive thinking, and athletes, speakers, soldiers and actors frequently use it to enhance their performances. Visualization practices are also a common form of spiritual exercise. In Vajrayana Buddhism, complex visualizations are a leg of the journey to Buddhahood.

There are a number of ways to use this process to gain clarity, but it's especially applicable to your relationship with your audience. Try visualizing your audience as being full of loving allies. Grammy-nominated saxophonist Dave Koz always thinks of an audience this way.

"They can't wait to love you. So, instead of gearing up worrying that people will hate you, remind yourself that they are just waiting to love you. Then, all you need is to go out there and just be yourself. If you have that confidence going in, it makes jumping off the cliff easier because you know that they're there with the net. You have to really, really screw it up big time to not have that."

ACTION STEP:
VISUALIZE

Mission

Close your eyes and spend one minute breathing in for five seconds and then breathing out for five seconds. Continue breathing slowly and conjure up images of people you love and who love you. Imagine these people are the audience of your presentation, loving everything you say or do. Now imagine everyone in the real audience loving everything you say or do. Imagine that that audience really needs to get every ounce of information you are providing; it's a lifeline they can't live without. You are critical to their success and existence. Own and absorb their appreciation and love for you.

Sian Beilock writes about visualization in her book, Choke: *What the Secrets of the Brain Reveal About Getting It Right When You Have To*. She points out that sports trainers often suggest that athletes associate thoughts of love and family with the adrenaline rush they get with performance. It reduces their chances of choking, because instead of associating that adrenaline with reasons to fail, they associate it with positive thoughts.

Dr. Richard Bandler models the conscious and unconscious patterns unique to each of us in such a way that we are continuously moving toward a higher potential.[4] His neuro-linguistic programming (NLP) creates change in people, particularly as they respond to and utilize what they think (neuro), what they say (linguistic) and what they do (programming). And the process is all about visualization.

I have had some positive experiences using NLP techniques from motivational speaker Tony Robbins. In one, I think of a happy memory, note how I feel about it and then make it bigger and brighter in my mind.

The general function behind this, other than mood control, is to accomplish goals. You visualize yourself achieving a particular objective, and focus on that visualization until you have achieved it in real life. In theory, this allows you to focus on that particular goal more fully and achieve it more

---

[4] Sue Knight, *NLP At Work: The Difference That Makes a Difference in Business* (Boston: Nicholas Brealey Publishing, 1999).

readily.

Lindsey Agness in her book, Change Your Life with NLP, writes that the conscious mind is the goal setter and the unconscious mind is the goal getter. The key to this is the reticular activating system that allows your unconscious mind to achieve whatever you put your conscious mind to. This is why a key phrase in NLP is "be careful what you focus on," because it will manifest itself, whether positive or negative.

Claude Bristol was a forerunner to all of this back in the 1940s, expanding on 19th-century New Thought principles to suggest that there is intelligence in everything that exists in the universe. In his book, The Magic of Believing, he argued that we're all linked by a universal mind.

Psychiatrist Carl Jung had a similar idea: collective unconscious. He thought the beliefs of individuals were quantifiable and could directly impact the minds of other people and even inanimate objects. The more powerful your "broadcast," the more likely the world would pick it up and react accordingly.

Astrophysicist Sir Arthur Eddington was sure that the physical laws of the universe could be influenced by human thought. Some scientists think that modern quantum physics supports this belief, as well. Bristol's explanation is that a person with a strong belief exists at a certain vibration that seeks its like in the form of matter. Thus, the startling conclusion: You do not achieve deep-felt goals by action alone, but are helped along depending on the quality and intensity of the belief that they will be achieved.

Chapter 7: Re-Mind

What does all this science I'm citing mean to us? My mentor Jim Samuels has used it to create a process he calls Re-minding. It takes all my positive and negative thoughts and helps me use them to my advantage, and it ultimately creates—you guessed it—clarity. Re-minding incorporates the best parts of visualization, NLP and the laws of attraction in a simple, quick and effective process to transform the way you think about any undesirable experience—past, present or future.

Re-minding is also great fun. It frees you from bothersome or disturbing memories or fears and releases your natural optimism and energy. It has allowed me to change my mind and get excited about things that, moments prior, scared me. It also frees you from stress, fear, guilt, anger and any other debilitating feelings. It releases your natural motivation and instills you with optimism about your future. Jim has written a book, *Re-mind Yourself*, that I highly recommend. Here is a concise version of the process.[5]

ACTION STEP:
REMIND YOURSELF (I)

Mission
1. **Clarify the issue.** *I'm about to give a speech to a group of students, and I'm afraid that they will find me boring and uncool.*
2. **Capture it in your imagination.** *I'm giving the speech, and I see kids looking at their phones, yawning and talking to their neighbors.*
3. **Convert that into a Re-minder by greatly exaggerating some aspect of it.** *They yawn so much that they melt, and all that's left are puddles with vibrating phones.*

At this point, I'm laughing out loud. From now on, when I think of giving a speech to students—or anyone else who I thought would find me boring and uncool—this Re-minder will influence my perception, and my feelings will be different. This change is subconscious, as well. It'll be part of me during all my speaking gigs from now on.

---

[5] Jim Samuels, PhD, *Re-Mind Yourself And Set Yourself Free* (CreateSpace, March 2012).

Mission

1. ***Clarify the issue.*** *I blow everyone away with how engaging, funny, clever and imaginative my speech is.*

2. ***Capture it in your imagination.*** *I'm onstage, totally confident, watching the students' faces as they light up with enthusiasm and laugh at every joke. I'm confident from their expressions and responses that their lives are changing. The speech ends with a standing ovation.*

3. ***Convert that into a Re-minder by greatly exaggerating some aspect of it.*** *I grow to 100 feet tall and pop through the ceiling. I hear the crashing and breaking of the concrete, steel and wood as my head breaks through, but there's no pain. The crowd below is going wild, cheering and yelling in joy, and I pick up the tiny school principal with my two fingers as he hands me a check for $1 million.*

Re-minding dramatically changes the way you think about, act and respond to whatever situation you're in. This is the stuff that changes you at the molecular level, rerouting your brain and building neuro-networks that alter the way you think about something permanently. The performance anxiety dissipates and is replaced by clarity to focus on the presentation. Bingo!

Chapter 8: Understand Your Fear

Jerry Seinfeld has a quote: "According to most studies, people's No. 1 fear is public speaking. No. 2 is death. Death is No. 2. Does that sound right? This means to the average person, if you go to a funeral, you're better off in the casket than doing the eulogy."

Have you heard the acronym F.E.A.R. (False Evidence Appearing Real)? Misinterpreting fear as an illusion or lie is dangerous (though one interviewee for this book uses F.E.A.R. in a context that is totally appropriate). Fear can be a reaction to an illusion we've created in our mind. But it's the belief that's key here. If we think our illusions are real, then the reactions are real and need to be treated as such.

Fear as an emotional reaction to something threatening is appropriate—a car careens toward you, someone holds a gun to your head. This isn't false evidence; it's factual evidence, and fear is designed to preserve your life. In other words, there are times when you should be afraid. In the context of this book, once you are clear on your goal, you need to set realistic expectations of what you want to achieve so your capability level is appropriate. Define your intended competence as specifically as you can. Align your expectations with reality. In other words, make sure that your expectations about your presentation, communication or performance are realistic and based on your actual competency.

Zappos CEO Tony Hsieh refers to the book *Confessions of a Public Speaker* by Scott Berkun, who says it's all about evolution. "Ten thousand years ago, if you had 500 pairs of eyes on you and your back was against the wall, it was a very, very bad thing. Now, if you're in this situation, you're a leader; back then you were dead."

Erik Weihenmayer relies on his mind's eye, since he can't see with his real ones. "On one side you have the adventure of life and the excitement and the fun and the thrill—and on the other side you have the fear. You have the positive stuff pulling you one way, and the fear pulling you the other way. It's then a question of which one is more powerful."

Erik remembers how terrified he was the first time he climbed the Khumbu Icefall. "I remember waking up early. I had a cup of coffee in my hand, and my hand was shaking like crazy. I couldn't even hold the cup—you know how when you're so scared you can't pick things up. You pick something up, and it drops out of your hands, and you're just losing your coordination. I remember thinking, 'Wow, I can't even function. I can't even tie a knot.'"

But there's a point at which you're as ready as you're ever going to be. And at that point, Erik says, fear can only sabotage you. "You've prepared; you've done everything you can. You're ready. This is your moment. At that point, all those fears and doubts start to pour through your brain, because your brain wants to protect you. It's a mechanism left over from when we were cavemen. That fear protects you from walking out and getting eaten by a saber-toothed tiger.

Just like Berkun says.

"It short-circuits you. It says, 'Get off the mountain. Go down to the sunshine and sidewalks and hamburgers. What are you doing?' You just have to accept that that's the way the brain functions. It's calling you away from adventure."

If Erik had listened to his brain, he would never have summited Mount Everest. He's learned to take his fear and transmute it into focus and awareness—a hyper-awareness of his surroundings. Clarity.

"There's a really cool Tibetan quote that I heard when I was on Everest, 'The nature of the mind is like water; if you do not disturb it, it will become clear.' Your mind can fill up with all these distractions—all these fears and doubts trying to pull you away. You over-think. So, when I'm climbing and I'm freaked out, I go into a Zen state, where I'm more awareness and focus than mud and distraction. Here's an example: If I'm going into a massive rock with a whitewater kayak, my friends are talking to me via these radios, and they align my kayak up exactly right. But if we are a foot off or if the angle is just slightly off, I'm going to get hammered. So, when I'm going into that situation, I just keep my mind still, like water."

He also listens to the advice of his friends, especially Chris Morris who taught him to "con his brain." Erik could either focus on the enormity of the mountain and the failings of the human body...or focus on the possibilities.

"I forced myself to sit outside my tent and envision myself crossing ladders—doing things right, going through the motions correctly in my brain. Ultimately, I'd see myself standing on the summit with my team. In my mind, I'd hear the flags blowing, we'd be hugging, tears would be coming out, and I'd be like, 'Wow, this is powerful.'" It's a lesson in positive, self-reinforcement, doing things right in your mind, first.

Erik also talks about his alchemy theory, turning the negative (lead) into the positive (gold). "There's a point where I felt that fear was no longer in control. 'You can totally panic here, but that isn't gonna help you coming down from a mountain in a massive storm, getting picked up and slammed back against a rock with your hands freezing. There are a million things going wrong. I could totally panic right now. What's that gonna do for me?' Out of necessity, I learned to take that potentially uncontrollable panicky thing that happens in my brain, and translate it into a sense of hyperawareness. I'm here, and I can do no wrong! This is a 'Don't Fall Zone,' so I'm not gonna fall."

Erik keeps the focus on his goal. When you get caught up in distractions, you're actually concentrating on all of the things that can derail and undermine your true purpose. Erik has developed the ability to translate his panic into hyperawareness out of necessity, because he's in life and death situations. It's pretty humbling to compare my performance anxiety to falling down the side of a mountain. Having said that, fear of any kind can still seem insurmountable, even if the actual consequences are not life threatening. This is why processes like Re-minding can be so effective, getting us to laugh at our fears and forge ahead with true goals without creating panic about everything that can go wrong.

Chapter 9: Get Some Serious Focus

Recognizing the high-anxiety job of U.S. football kicker, I spoke with three: Chicago Bear Robbie Gould, free agent Clint Stitser and former Fresno State Bulldog Kevin Goessling. I also spoke with John Baxter, current University of Southern California special teams coach, who coached both Clint and Kevin. Each one gave me a different perspective on clarity and visualization as it applies to sports performance. Clint also gave me some interesting ideas about how his experience as a professional football player has improved his sales ability as the owner of a real estate business.

Let's start with Goessling, who uses visualization now, but hasn't always. He remembers his first collegiate home game with Fresno State against the University of Wisconsin. He was one-for-four on field goals—one hit the upright, another barely missed and the third shanked pretty hard. Fresno ended up losing, 10-13. Goessling was a redshirt freshman, and he was feeling pressure from all sides.

Goessling's next home appearance was a conference game against Hawaii; he went three-for-three until the Warriors blocked a kick, sending the game into overtime. He missed a 35-yarder, and Hawaii won by three. Two home games, two home losses, both of which he could have prevented.

It was do or go home, so Goessling called a sports psychologist before a road game at Utah State. The doc's advice: You don't have to kick a great ball every time. It just has to be a good one. He told Goessling to find a focal point—an attribute on the field or one of the uprights or the 50-yard line—something, anything, that he could find every week, no matter where he was playing. That would be his restart button to help him refresh. So, he starts his routine fresh every kick, no matter the success of the last one, no matter his location on the field.

His first field goal against Utah State was a short, 22-yarder and he missed. His next opportunity didn't arrive until less than eight minutes remained in the fourth quarter: 43 yards. It sailed in. Several (football) minutes later from 44 yards out: good. With two seconds left, the Utah coach tried to ice him by calling a timeout. Goessling restarted his routine, went out, took his steps, found his target and made it—setting the school record for distance (58 yards), but more importantly, leading Fresno State to the win.

"It felt great because twice already that season, people tried to say that we lost the game because of a kick that I missed. Now, we won a game because of three kicks in a row that I made."

Coach John Baxter remembers that kick. "The pressure on him was immense. He went into class, and other students booed him. He had a brick thrown through his apartment window. I said, 'Lord, no person ever deserves this amount of pain.' I couldn't even imagine his life, his psyche, had he missed that kick. During the timeout, I waved to him. I said, 'Kevin come here.' And he sloughed me.

"I went out, I grabbed him and I said, 'You get over here right now, OK? Don't ever slough me, because right now, the only person who believes that you can do this is standing right next to you. No. 1: You're at 7,000 feet. This ball's gonna travel. No. 2: Look at the flag.' And he turned around, and looked at it. It was straight at his back. I said, 'All you have to do is pick a target. If you trust your target, you're gonna make it.'"

The wind, the elevation, everything was right for the perfect kick. And Baxter played the role of a coach, someone who takes you where you can't take yourself. "Sometimes the instruction is technical, sometimes the instruction is emotional. Sometimes it's spiritual. You fill in where you need to fill in."

Coach Baxter utilizes F.E.A.R. in a practical way. He asks his athletes to visualize how they would play, practice and participate if they knew nothing could go wrong.

"When parents worry about kids, their imaginations are running wild, thinking of all the things that could go wrong. When coaches worry about their players, they're thinking about all the things that could go wrong. When players worry about their performance, they're thinking about all of the things that could go wrong. And that's the exact wrong place to be. The last thing you want is someone over-analyzing a situation."

Baxter takes his players through a ritual. On Fridays, they do a walk-through. That night, they all watch film. They get written tips and reminders to memorize, and they stand up and recite them. On Saturday mornings, they do another walk-through. They rehearse and rehearse and rehearse. They slow it down, so that when they're in game-time situations, they react on instinct.

They focus on their goal and engage in complete clarity about what they need to do. Baxter helps them eliminate distractions, considerations, ambiguities and false evidence by replacing it with clear vision.

Clint played for Baxter, too. And he relies on strict visualization techniques that not only enable him to focus as a pro athlete, but as the head of his residential real estate business.

"For me it's an outcome-based obsession [clarity of goal]. I build a tunnel to my target. I walk the field anytime I have the opportunity. Even when I'm driving on the freeway, I focus on the big light pole a mile ahead. I practice funneling all of my emotions and energy down the line right into that light pole. There can be all these things going on around me, whether it's a stadium going nuts, a baby crying, whatever it is, and I just practice mastering all of my emotions and energies funneled right to my target."

Remember, real clarity gives you the focus and motivation to solve problems and cut through all distractions.

"I don't care where my head position is. I don't care how my body does it. Harnessing the energy keeps me from being mentally weak and becoming afraid—or letting the situation take control. I do this by associating pain with weakness. I've worked on the associative techniques, and I'm associating pain with being unfocused and pleasure with being focused."

Clint is about results. That's why he plays golf. He goes out to the driving range where he can practice controlling his emotions and focusing his energy.

Here is how visualization—and the quest for clarity—applies to his business life. Residential real estate is an emotional transaction. Sellers have poured their hearts and money into homes that in today's market may be going for substantially less than their investment. Buyers are purchasing based on their dreams for the future. Transactions can take months. Emotions are high, and people can say or do things they don't mean.

"When it comes down to a key negotiation with a bank or a seller or meeting a certain requirement for a loan, you don't want to allow any 'noise' that's occurred over the previous six to eight months to hinder your decision-making process to execute your portion of the deal. I employ that tunnel vision, because there's a point when you could easily sit there and point fingers back and forth and battle one another.

"All this noise can kill the deal. What you can do is bring everything back to basics and focus on the simple objective. I have to do that on a day-to-day basis, and you have to hold people's hands in that process to help control their emotions. The football in front of me is gonna be funneled right down this hallway I've built. All my emotions and energy are going right there in a positive way. The inhibiting thoughts that create fear are no longer part of me."

Clint has a thought process (he calls it a modality of concentration). It's directed, it's positive and it coheres to his body's personality. All the negative thoughts that are based on uncertainty never show up.

"If you let your mind create enough evidence to make fear appear real, then you can be debilitated by it. At the same time, your mind can also create enough evidence to focus and create the goal that you want. You can either let emotions cripple you or you can harness them."

Clint talks about the distraction of the video screen at M&T Bank Stadium in Baltimore. It's behind the uprights, right where a kicker might look. There's his big face.

"When you're picking a target, and it's a close-up of you; it can really screw you up. So, you have to pick something either below or above it. When I build that tunnel, stupid stuff like that no longer becomes a factor. I'm zoned into my target with laser vision. The holder takes his spot, and I give him a reassuring pat on the head or a high five, just to build a little extra rapport in the moment. I take a deep breath; I just do a natural release. I've been doing it long enough to where I've even found what release works best for me."

Clint most recently kicked for the UFL's Las Vegas Locomotives under coach Jim Fassel, who isn't known as tight-lipped when it comes to playing hard. "If someone's not doing their job, he'll just fire you, like right away. He doesn't care who you are. If you're not doing your job in practice, he'll yell, 'Give me a new left tackle!' Every year he fires at least two kickers before he settles on one.

If one performance can jeopardize your entire career, you're a prime candidate for performance anxiety—and the need for clarity. "At one point I envisioned Superman with his laser vision melting stuff. I had to get in the zone so intently that I had two lasers coming out of my eyes that went right to the target. It helps me set the mentality of being the aggressor and not the aggressee."

Victoria Recaño, an Emmy award-winning presenter, best known as correspondent and host of *The Insider*, recently filmed a soliloquy in a movie—and blanked.

"I was freaking out. I've never had that happen. I had no idea what the line was. It blows your whole confidence, and suddenly it feels like you're choking. Thankfully, the director was really nice. And he actually talked me through it."

But she doesn't blank often. Victoria actually uses a little curio to remind her of her clarity—which comes from faith. "I say this prayer with this little plastic thing with a Sacred Heart of Jesus on it that the nuns gave all of us in school as kids. I had that when I anchored at ZDTV [later TechTV], because I was so stressed out when I first started. I had no idea that I was going to be the anchor. I thought I was just coming in to be a correspondent."

She remembers asking who the co-anchor would be, and her surprise/horror when they responded that there wouldn't be one.

"Of course, I freaked, and I called up this woman who I used to work with in St. Louis, and she suggested that I find something that will always be a symbol to channel all the stress into. If you watch the old shows, I always have that in my hand. Eventually, you don't necessarily need it anymore. But I had it physically there for six years. Now, it's there metaphorically."

ACTION STEP:
CREATE AN ANCHOR

Mission
Find something (or someone) that you can focus on at the beginning of your pre-performance routine to clear everything else out of your mind. This anchor represents your routine. Use it to channel your anxiety and gain clarity. Associate this anchor with the strength and focus of your pre-performance ritual or routine.

Chapter 10: Find the Fortitude of Gratitude

"As we express our gratitude, we must never forget that the highest appreciation is not to utter words, but to live by them." —John F. Kennedy

A few months back, my 2 year old, Zade, and my wife, Lisa, were lying in our garden. Lisa said, "Zade, you are so beautiful."

Zade answered, "Mommy, you are so beautiful."

Lisa responded, "Thank you, Zade. And what about daddy? Is he beautiful, too?"

Zade said, "No, daddy is not beautiful. Daddy is thankful."

Anyone who knows me well knows I'm all about gratitude. I focus on everything I have, and gratitude for all that fortifies my thoughts. This mental endorsement gives me clarity as it relates to my goal which is directly strengthened by focusing on what's in my glass rather than what's not. This helps me fixate on my strengths. The more I focus on my strengths, the more I fortify my clarity which dictates the action I need to take (capability) and drives me to confidence.

My publisher, Tim Sanders (bestselling author, speaker and former Yahoo! chief solutions officer), quotes his grandma, Billye: "Gratitude is a muscle, not a feeling. You've got to give your gratitude muscle a workout every day if you want to feel grateful."[6]

So, Tim exercises his gratitude muscle by waking up thankful. It sets the tone for the entire day—directing his subconscious to notice desirable things. He focuses on three people he's grateful for, saying their names and their contributions. This gives him an immediate sense of confidence, because he knows he's not alone. I've tried it, and it's quite effective in relaxing my mind and clearing out negative thoughts that distract me. Tim says, "The difference between a grateful person and an ungrateful person lies in perception. One sees a life of beauty, and the other sees a life of lack."

Years ago, I discovered that I can't have a positive and negative thought in my mind at the same time. If I shift my thoughts to something desirable, the negative thoughts disperse. I decided to learn how to do this on command in order to thrive in moments of anxiety or stress. Now, I do this with gratitude.

---

[6] Tim Sanders, *Today We Are Rich: Harnessing the Power of Total Confidence* (Tyndale House Publishers Inc., October 2012).

Sometimes it takes great focus, and sometimes it comes easily. Either way, if I'm committed, then it works, especially before a presentation or performance. It's a quick way to rake away the anxiety.

I remember a celebratory boat party with Cher, the band, dancers and crew—nearly 100 people in all. It wasn't a celebration of anything in particular, just our general accomplishments as a team. It was in the middle of what turned out to be the longest recorded tour for a female artist in pop music history—just five weeks short of three years.

I will remember forever a conversation I had with Cher, looking into her big brown Cher eyes, watching her long black Cher hair blow in the wind, listening to her classic Cher voice and smelling her signature Cher perfume (Uninhibited). I asked her to what she attributes her success—"gratitude," she said.

P!NK relies on gratefulness, too. Back in 2007 in Dubai, the band, dancers and singers enjoyed some indoor snow skiing at 25 degrees Fahrenheit, before heading out to lunch on the beach in 120-degree heat. We took a walk afterward when P!NK suddenly stopped and said, "OK, everyone, I want you all to tell me three things you're grateful for right now!"

It was an easy time to bolster gratitude, sure, but that's when it occurred to me that success is the result of a successful mindset. There's an abundance of successful people who use gratitude as a tool to foster achievement, as opposed to simply being grateful when success happens. I've had more successful performances as a result of exercising the gratitude muscle than I can count.

Now, every night, before we go on stage with P!NK, we get into a gratitude circle. She talks about everything she's grateful for, and you can feel the energy rise as everyone gets into it. We start celebrating what we have. It's a gratitude party. She talks about being thankful for her career, her health, her voice, her family, bones and limbs that still work—the humor she finds in all of us dorks surrounding her. We remind each other to be thankful.

You need clarity when you use this technique. Start with little things, and see what happens. Before you know it, your negative feelings are gone. Remember: Positive and negative thoughts cannot occur simultaneously. As author Peter McWilliams says, "You can't afford the luxury of a negative thought."

I have one last gratitude story. We had just flown to Germany for the last leg of P!NK's 2007 tour, which had exceeded everyone's expectations. The first show was in Hamburg the night after we arrived. I loved the show, and I was looking forward to a peaceful and restful sleep. As we are leaving the venue for the hotel, Alecia (aka P!NK) told us that she wanted to meet for a drink at the bar at midnight. I was exhausted, but if the boss wants to meet for a drink, I'll be there.

We all showed up. The mood was festive. We were an integrated and synergistic group and everyone enjoyed each other's company. I was tired, but happy. I was about to retire for the evening after one drink, when Alecia stood up and announced that she wanted to play a drinking game, and if the boss wants to play a drinking game, then I'll play a drinking game.

She said the game was called B.D.G. (brag, desire, gratitude). It did not sound like a drinking game, but I knew Alecia wasn't one for the traditional liver-challenging activity. The game went like this: Each one of us had to share something we were proud of (brag), something we wanted (desire) and something we were thankful for (gratitude). Some of us excelled at it, others retreated. I found it intriguing, especially under the guise of a drinking game.

Three hours later, we were still in the bar. We had been laughing, crying and hugging. It turned out to be one of the most inspiring, cathartic and unifying experiences I've ever had, and that includes weekend spiritual retreats and self-improvement seminars.

I've since employed this process in seminars and witnessed some amazing results. I changed the name to B.A.G. (brag, aspiration, gratitude) to make it a bit more memorable. After a bit of research into why this "drinking game" was so effective, I determined the following. Most of us are taught not to brag, but when we get to acknowledge our accomplishments, especially publicly, it reinforces our strengths. It also gives people insights into what you care about. Then, when you tell people your aspirations, you're clarifying your goals publicly. This makes them more real for you and gives your peeps a chance to support and endorse the things that you want to accomplish. I've already explained the power of gratitude.

So, here is an effective action step that I've seen work for rockers, corporate leaders, students and at-risk youth. It will give you power, clarity and reduce your anxiety. This exercise is intended for a group or for an individual. Keep it in the context of an upcoming presentation, performance or communication. If you're alone, talk out loud.

Mission

Brag about something that you have accomplished that really means a lot to you. Define an aspiration or goal. Focus on something powerful that you're grateful for.

Chapter 11: The Highest Good for All Concerned

I like to focus on the highest good for all concerned (as opposed to just my concern), and it's my responsibility to have clarity not only for myself, but for those who rely on it. This clarity of details, communication, job description, timing and appropriateness can make the difference between being world class or second class.

Of course, your core competency (capability) is paramount to the effectiveness of your team's performance. Once you have clarity, it's on you to show up and perform to your maximum capability. The more capability you demonstrate, the more confidence others will have in you, which reduces your (potential) anxiety.

In performing for the highest good for all concerned, you're doing your part to derail anxiety and resulting fallout by taking full responsibility for creating your own confidence. If you want to be of additional service, coach your group in the three Cs.

One of the great luxuries of life and learning is that the more we know, the more we can be responsible for. By exhibiting and communicating a calming and confident disposition, you can affect the entire group with proactive energy, thought and intention—especially when others may be infecting it with reactive, nervous energy and dis-ease. Be the great stabilizer.

Chapter 12: Know Your Role

Like I've said before, it all begins with clarity. And clarifying even the smallest details can add a deeper level of subtlety to a group's performance. P!NK's manager, Roger Davies, always says, "Now remember, lots of animation everybody, lots of animation."

It's funny to think about that as it relates to my most recent tour with Foreigner, when we made a point to always engage the audience. I became more and more animated as the tour progressed, standing up behind my drum kit, frequently throwing sticks into the audience, and generally taking on a very audacious stage persona. Well, when I joined back up with P!NK, I sensed the need to curve my visual antics—tame the rock 'n' roll beast just a bit, keeping the energy high, but choosing my moments to express more or less flare. I'm still finding that balance, but I'm sure that it will be what's best for the tour and P!NK.

Sometimes we're in situations we're not prepared for, but our presence or teamwork is paramount to success. Clarify your importance. When you own that value, it makes you more confident.

Wings drummer Denny Seiwell shared a story about Linda McCartney: It was the early 1970s, and it was a really tough time for her. The press was unrelenting in its criticism, saying that she broke up the Beatles, pointing out every out-of-tune note. During the band's first European tour, Denny remembers that Linda just wanted to be back on the farm with her kids and the animals, just being a mom. But she was her husband's muse.

"Paul needed her there. If she wasn't there, I don't think we would have done Wings. I mean, she kicked him out of the house in Scotland and said, 'Get off your ass. You're a music maker; you're a writer; you're an artist. Let's go make a record.' He would have stayed up there and drank and just hung out because he was so tired of what he was going through, suing the other three Beatles and all."

It was clear to Denny that Linda had a strong purpose—just being there. The first night of the tour, backstage and afraid, she turned to him for advice, and he reminded her that it simply wasn't about her.

"I said, 'It doesn't matter what you did or what you do, we're not here for you. You're part of our band, and you're part of your old man. He needs you here. So, go out there and do as good as you can and smile.

"She couldn't smile. She couldn't do it. She thought she was really holding back her husband by being there. But she got it for that night. She hung in there as best she could until she finally adjusted to being up there. And we'd be playing, and I'd shoot her a look—'It's OK. Go for it. Have some fun. The mic's not even on.'"

Thank goodness for Linda's courage. R.I.P.!

ACTION STEP:
CLARIFY YOUR ROLE

Questions
1. *Why am I here?*
2. *What did I do to get to this point?*
3. *What is my value to this group?*
4. *What can I do to be of the greatest benefit?*
5. *What can I do to celebrate my position right now?*

SECTION 2: CAPABILITY

"The absent-minded maestro was racing up New York's 7th Avenue to a rehearsal, when a stranger stopped him. 'Pardon me,' the stranger said. 'Can you tell me how to get to Carnegie Hall?' 'Yes,' answered the maestro breathlessly. 'Practice!'" —E.E. Kenyon's syndicated column "The Wit Parade"

Capability represents preparation, education, the proper feeding of the mind and the proper execution of skills. When I started writing this book, I had little experience interviewing people, but I was clear that I wanted to obtain stories and information.

My capability developed with every interview, as I clarified what I needed to improve in the content of my questions, how I articulated that content, how I listened to the answers, how I took mental notes for follow-up questions and even how I could best technically capture the content (recording, backing up and editing).

And I started with a friend—Foreigner singer Kelly Hansen—since I was on the road with him at the time. It was a wonderful learning opportunity for me, and, frankly, I wasn't so much nervous as unfamiliar and awkward.

Looking back, Kelly was super easy on me as I stumbled through that interview at a conference table in his Ft. Pierce, Fla., hotel suite before a show. Aptly, his advice to overcome nerves was preparation.

Being a successful lead singer is all about prep work, and he does that. But live, national TV gigs still scare the bejesus out of him, not only because of the huge audience, but also because of the event's longevity on YouTube and reruns. "You can't get rid of it," he says.

So, he likes to know exactly what he's going to be doing, he talks to the people running the show and he gets all the logistics beforehand. "It's important that I understand everything that's going on and everything that's going to happen so that, in my mind, I have it set, and I'm prepared. Then I can prepare for any contingencies."

This preparation enables him to make better instantaneous decisions in the event of a misstep. He's been preparing for those mistakes for years. His first question: Is this something that the audience is going to really recognize? If no, he's trained himself to fight the natural inclination to scowl or show embarrassment or anger.

"If it's something that you know, absolutely, the audience saw, like if you tripped over a stage prop and you fell, then you make it entertaining. You turn it into something comical or funny. Once you do that, you move on. You can't drag it out. You can't keep talking about it. You have to get past it and move on."

If you're starting a company, a job, a product or a project, begin your journey by expanding your knowledge base relevant to the task at hand. Your preparation needs to be as great as your vision for success. My father, Dr. Benson Schulman, earned a doctorate in English composition and grammar and wrote four college-level English books while teaching full time and supporting our family. He also had shelves upon shelves of science fiction and reference books. His passion for knowledge made him a voracious reader and a successful teacher, author and father.

Remember, it's imperative to clarify what competence means to you. You need to define specifically how capable you really are. Capability is capability, and nothing is substitute. The more you mix in other things, the more you obscure the simplicity of being capable. If someone challenges you or asks if you're sure you can do something, you know you can. Someone could splash water on you at 4 a.m., and you could get up and do it. That gives you confidence. You won't acknowledge any performance anxiety, because you know what to expect from your performance.

Chapter 13: Make Your Preparation Extreme

Author and speaker Tim Sanders inspired me to take even greater precaution in my preparation to ensure the highest level of capability.

Before he even gets on the plane to fly to a speaking gig, he's performed all the custom pieces of his presentation either directly in front of his client or, at the very least, staring himself down in the mirror. Even when he writes (he has two *New York Times* bestsellers), he rehearses. He plans out what he's going to pen, outlines it on a whiteboard, bullet-points the nuggets, visualizes the experience of writing it, records the composition and listens to it a couple of times.

At some point, he's ready. He turns everything off, runs downstairs to his studio and starts typing like a madman. Forty-five minutes later, he has 1,000 words of gold. The execution of writing is the delivery of art, he says.

He sees this preparation as vital—especially when the performance is live. He should know; one blown performance could end his speaking career—just like one bad outing from an NFL kicker. That's not to say he's never been part of a botched operation. As a former Yahoo exec, he recalls meetings when bad intelligence led him and his team to "split our jeans with a creative idea." In those situations, transparency is the best medicine. He described the poor intelligence, detailed what he had hoped to accomplish and admitted it was a stupid idea. Ask for the right information, so you can go back and re-conceive a solution.

That's why clarity should always start with research. Research means Tim knows the context of his performance really, really well—and that doesn't just mean its content. He researches the set and its colors; he researches his audience members, their perceptions and why they'll be in attendance; he researches the desired outcome of his stakeholders.

Invariably, he finds some nugget about the room or the company or the audience, something they think he doesn't know that he anticipates sharing. Every performance is different and tailored to each audience. Sameness is never good—your same-old-thing won't work for every crowd, and that can cause untold anxiety.

You also need to dismiss adversity by making it familiar. Like Mike Tyson says, the torque of a punch doesn't knock you out, the surprise does. Anticipate those surprise punches.

Tim was my second interview, and he inspired me to approach the rest of my interviews with greater clarity. I did extensive research not only on the backgrounds of my interviewees, but I anticipated what they might say so I could have alternate questions prepared. I also conducted follow-up interviews and emails to reinforce my content with greater detail. I did research on the environments where we would meet, and what the recording conditions would be.

This clarity and knowledge set me up well for interview No. 3—Jeremy Piven at super-trendy restaurant Caffe Primo on Sunset Boulevard in West Hollywood. I'm glad I upped my preparation with some better recording gear and a directional mic—super trendy also means super noisy. Jeremy looked a bit frazzled, like he was in the middle of a hectic day. He relaxed a bit as we ate, and we both had a good time.

Jeremy traces his reliance on preparation back to an incident during childhood theater camp, when, impromptu, he was given a set of notecards to read on stage during an intermission. "I just remember being very young and intimidated and seeing the words and panicking and just bombing in a terrifying way," he said. "It was a disaster, and it affected me pretty profoundly. It instilled in me an understanding that you need to be prepared."

Not just so you won't bomb. Jeremy likes to be present, and have the ability to take chances and be brave, and unless he's completely prepared, he can't do that. Preparation gives him that confidence to step out of his comfort zone, so the extraordinary can occur. "People can sense when you're confident and present and in the moment and when you're crippled by fear. It's palpable."

Jeremy referenced a book that has had a big impact on him and is also in my arsenal—*Outliers* by Malcolm Gladwell. Gladwell writes that the key to success in any pursuit is practice, specifically 10,000 hours of practice. This is what creates mastery. Since the book's 2008 publication, the 10,000-hour rule has seen broad adoption.

I have learned to leverage the 10,000 hours I have in one area to bolster other areas. I use my 10,000 hours of drumming performance to help me as a speaker. I've developed a keen sense of timing, can read the audience and performers on stage, have the ability to perform in adverse and varying conditions and gained others skills that enhance my clarity and capability as a speaker.

Just because you haven't hit your 10,000 hours in public speaking or performing, doesn't mean you're going to fail. Jeremy practices his drumming as often as he can, but he also relies on professionals like me. One of his 10,000-hours-of-acting skills is taking direction. He's also a natural mimic. He has taken great direction from me when sitting in with my all-star band. He leverages his 10,000 hours of acting to support his 1,500 hours of drumming. And that preparation helps him during performances with what he calls "real musicians."

Situations can also arise that are unique and you need to draw upon your capability and instinct to help you navigate new territory. Consider Billy Hayes, a former police officer and retired NYC firefighter who was a first responder on Sept. 11, 2001. How did he focus in the aftermath of the terrorist attack? He drew on all the past events and experiences in his life. That preparation enabled him to focus and perform, to put the fear and panic behind him.

Touring with Foreigner last year, I had to play a free-form solo, and while I had my 10,000 drumming hours, I didn't have 10,000 free-form solo hours. The whole show would go by and that was the one tenuous moment for me. So, every available second, I clocked off those hours either practicing or mentally going over the drum parts in my head, which studies have shown can be very effective—but more on that later.

Leigh Gallagher, assistant managing editor of *FORTUNE* and TV/radio business commentator, shares her early experiences as a presenter. Producers would tell her the subject matter, and she would meticulously fill out index cards with her thoughts. "I just studied the hell out of all of the cards. I made sure I knew my case. In those early days, I would prepare six talking points, and the TV producer would look at me and laugh in my face. 'You get time to make one—and it better be three to six words long!'"

Leigh says a friend turned her on to a quote by former U.S. President Dwight D. Eisenhower: "Plans are worthless, but planning is everything." Great planning and just knowing your topic really well are the best ways to success.

"I used to play piano when I was growing up," she recalls. "My teacher used to say, 'You need to play it 18 times in a row without a single mistake in order to be able to play it once in front of people.'"

ACTION STEP:
PREPARE FOR PREPARATION

Mission

Outline the steps you need to go through to know you're prepared. Commit to repeating these steps until they're part of your "muscle memory." Practice until your know and do these by heart.

Chapter 14: Embrace Your Place:
Introverts and Extroverts

Preparation can cut through any prejudices you have about what you can or can't accomplish or who you can or can't become. And if you think that extroverts make better presenters, I'll bust that myth right now. Zappos CEO Tony Hsieh is a really mellow guy—and he used to believe the same thing.

"Before I got into speaking, I thought that people who were extroverted spoke better, but these aren't really related. Actually, it's a completely different skill set that you just learn over time."

Mark Papia, chief revenue officer of Connexity, agrees. Mark has sold a billion dollars in media, published and edited magazines and worked at celebrated companies such as Yahoo!, MySpace, Monster and FOX.

Mark thinks of himself as atypical in the sales world, because he considers himself an introvert. But he warns not to confuse the word introverted with the word shy.

"I'm not shy by any stretch of the imagination, but I am an introvert. I analyze everything. When I went into sales, I wasn't shy; I out-thought the competition."

"A lot of extroverts will show up, and they'll walk in with a big smile and take you out for a nice meal. Then, they talk a whole bunch about the basketball game and then lay out the business program. Extroverts are awesome people. In fact, most of the sales people who have worked for me over the years have been extroverts.

"My process was a little different. I've always believed in analyzing the client's marketing mix so extensively that when I go to pitch somebody, I know their businesses as well as they do. I know where the opportunities are, and when I build a sales program for them, I feel confident that when I go in and pitch, it's something that's going to resonate."

I imagine that the extrovert's social graces combined with the introvert's over-achievement would result in a super-capable presentation for any client. Mark gained his confidence as an introvert from his intense analysis and subsequent preparation.

"The fact that I was an introvert didn't scare me away from going into sales. It emboldened me."

Mark knows his presentation inside out—with or without his media. "Sometimes, you're not sitting across the desk from a buyer, *mano-a-mano,* doing a pitch. Sometimes you're in front of 20 people in a conference room or 1,000 people in a ballroom."

Mark recalls a keynote for 2,000 at affiliate marketing company Commission Junction University. He showed up with his presentation on a flash drive, but there was something wrong with the system. The speech was pushed back 10, 15, 20 minutes.

"Finally the coordinator said to me, 'You know, I don't think we're going to get this fixed.' And I said, 'OK, what do you want to do?' And she said, 'Well, what do you mean? What are my options?' And I said, 'Well, do you want me to do the presentation anyway?' She said, 'How could you do the presentation anyway?' And I said, "Don't worry about that. Just get a bar stool and put it up on the stage and let's start the show.'

"She looked perplexed and said, 'You're going to do your presentation without your presentation?' And I said to her, 'When you've written every word of your presentation, presenting it without the presentation is a snap.'"

Just as he took the stage, management fixed the problem and his PowerPoint came up, but Mark was so confident in his preparation that it didn't matter.

"Whether I presented with a deck or without a deck, it would have been good, because I knew the presentation in and out. I analyze everything, and nothing finds its way into a presentation that I haven't thought about from three or four different standpoints."

Now, Mark's not implying that extroverts don't prepare as much, he's just suggesting that introverts can overcome their nerves through preparation.

Remember Dr. Sol Hamburg, the stutterer? He had a tremendous problem making phone calls. He could call his father at work, but he couldn't call his friends, because he couldn't get the words started. There was tremendous performance anxiety involved. "Are they going to hang up the phone on me—which happened many, many times. I wouldn't even try to get dates, because I couldn't get the conversation started."

So, Dr. Sol practiced in places he had the most difficulty performing. He'd sit with his speech therapist and call 411 (information) over and over, asking for phone numbers. He'd outline in his mind what he wanted to say. Even today, when he sees a new patient, he's already thought out what he's trying to get across.

Dr. Sol is one of the most confident communicators I know. He is articulate, intelligent and bold—a far cry from that scared, stuttering boy.

Chapter 15: Lead With Your Strengths

Build your confidence further by concentrating on your strengths and recalling—in those moments of performance anxiety—the work you've done. Even people who have capability can allow their confidence to falter when they lose focus on exactly what they're best at and where they've spent the most time clocking the hours.

In his book, *StrengthsFinder 2.0*, Tom Rath wrote, "People who do have the opportunity to focus on their strengths every day are six times as likely to be engaged in their jobs and more than three times as likely to report having an excellent quality of life."

Focusing on what you do best and what you have rehearsed the most is an obvious way to build your confidence. It's similar to your "brag" from the last chapter, and it can be an empowering reminder of the strength of your foundation. During defining moments, make the decision to focus on your strengths, the capability that afforded you to be in this position in the first place.

This is musician-turned-entrepreneur David Kalt's *modus operandi*. He lets his excitement for a topic take over. David doesn't focus on the analytical world of raw numbers, hypotheticals and analytics. He wants investors to see his dream, the vision of what he wants to build and where he wants to take the company. "I have a CFO that can do the other things."

When David tried to adapt to the world of numbers, he became really intimidated and felt he didn't have much strength.

The world of anxiety is not the "real" world. Anxiety is distortion. That's not where we want to live. Our natural state is not a state of anxiety; it's a state of focus and calm. When you're anxious or fearful, that's your fight or flight state. That's only appropriate when you are in basic survival mode. Assuming that your basic survival needs are taken care of, when you are in presentation mode, anxiety and fear are usually unnecessary and inappropriate.

David recalls a dominant business partner he really struggled with. They fought, a lot. They had trouble communicating.

"I actually had to figure out how I was going to deal with him and my anxiety around him. I realized that in order for me to succeed in that business relationship, I had to figure out how to play to my strengths and how to be in offensive mode.

David stepped down as CEO several years later and discussed the situation with his former partner.

"The chemistry between us made the company unique, but my memories are of fighting and bickering. Some of that anxiety did bring about greatness, but only as I figured out more techniques to better communicate and control my emotions. I gradually started to figure out how not to wear my emotions on my sleeve, how to be much more in control. One of the things that people tell me in business, and in personal life, is that I don't have a whole lot of filters—and you'll find that with passionate people. I had to figure out how to have better control of my communication and emotions in ways that would raise my game."

David thinks of performance anxiety like a habit you can let go. "A food habit, a smoking habit, a communication habit—fear or anxiety, that's a habit and you have to say you don't want to be like that."

I'm a musician, and musicians love to party. But partying for me isn't about drugs or alcohol; rather it's a state of mind—one of release, happiness and playing full out. Getting in that groove is far easier when you're doing something you know you're good at. Develop a method that works for you, and do it when the potential for anxiety arises.

Former Fresno State kicker Kevin Goessling consciously reminds himself to be confident. "Whether it's a field goal, a drum roll, whatever it is, you've done it so many times, you've practiced it and your body is not going to forget how to do it. The only thing that will really affect that is your mind getting in the way by trying to micromanage."

To put that busy mind at ease, Kevin addresses his thoughts: "Thank you very much. I hear what you're saying. I'm going to kick now."

It was special teams coach John Baxter who inspired Kevin to trust his instincts, telling him that the human body doesn't understand negative words. As parents of a young child, my wife and I have make this a cornerstone of our approach—we remind Zade of what she can do rather than what she can't.

Kevin cites one of his favorite books, *The Inner Game of Tennis*, which describes Self 1 (the teller) and Self 2 (the doer). "You've got to make Mind A let Mind B do the work," he says. "I just have to remind myself that my mind isn't what's kicking the ball. It's just giving me a couple of cues.

"I'm teaching my brain to understand what it doesn't know and what it doesn't control. If I try to control what's out of my control, then I'm just going to screw myself up. If you can control it, you don't have to worry about it, and if you can't control it, then don't worry about it. So either way, no worries."

I learned many years ago to treat that dubious inner voice like a small rebellious child. Just because my mind kicks up negative thoughts, doesn't mean I have to believe them. Like Kevin, I talk back. "Thank you for your input and comments, but I'm going to do what I have trained so thoroughly to do. OK Mind, have a nice day and talk to you later!"

It sounds a bit crazy, and it may look a bit crazy if someone's watching, but my spirit is guiding me, and that's the real me. The mind can chatter away and have tantrums—especially mine—but I never take it too seriously. Address it. That will quiet the chatter and give you more clarity. My mentor, Jim Samuels, calls it giving your mind a "receipt."

Kickers are such solitary figures in an otherwise team sport. That's what Clint Stitser learned before his intro to the pro sport on Dec. 5, 2010, when the Bengals played against the defending champion New Orleans Saints.

"The Bengals coach basically explained to me before the game that there's no loyalty to kickers in the industry. You're a hired gun, and if you miss your target, well, you're fired and that's just the way it is. You better accept it, and if you can channel those emotions, good for you; if you can't, you're probably not going to last very long."

Essentially, Clint had to acknowledge that, accept it and have confidence in the kicker he trained to be. He went three-for-three on field goals before he missed an extra point kick (PAT).

"I missed a point after touchdown in an NFL game, which for a rookie kicker is career suicide! I came to the sideline and I was frustrated, upset. At that point, guys on the team essentially no longer talk to you because they assume they're not going to see you anymore.

"So, I'm sitting on the sidelines with the knowledge that, at some point in time, I'm probably gonna have to go back in again. The only thing that I can do is just let go. I absolutely have to perform, or for sure I'm gonna be gone, and I'll never get a shot again. You miss a PAT again, and you're axed regardless. It's insurmountable.

"I feel like crap, and the coach of the Bengals is well known for riding players. He's in your face, in your ear screaming at you. He'll be yelling at you for something in the first quarter that happened four kicks ago, and he'd still be upset about it and asks to see pictures of it from the printers on the sidelines."

Oh, I should also mention that Clint's wife was in the stands. She was five-and-a-half months pregnant with their first child. He could have ridden that situation into serious meltdown. But he didn't. He took a deep breath, and realized that this could be one of the biggest comebacks of his career.

"There were times in college when we would lose a game, and the coach would use the phrase 'draw a line in the sand.' It was time to make a decision. So, I dragged my foot along the big white sideline and drew a line in the sand. 'I'm making a comeback, and I'm just going to let go. Screw it. I can't be paralyzed by this, because I've trained too hard to be this way.' The next time we got sent out on the field for a PAT it was good, and later I kicked a 47-yard field goal. But I'll never forget that point in my career when I was most vulnerable, right there on the sidelines, for the 10 or 15 minutes after that missed PAT, knowing that I might never go back in."

From the business perspective, Leigh Gallagher of *FORTUNE* gets more nervous speaking in person than she ever does on television. For her, TV is like being at a dinner party, where everyone shares their thoughts on a topic. Live speaking is a different animal all together. So, she reminds herself of one simple, powerful point.

"Someone decided that I belong on that stage and that I have something to say to these people. That's what you have to keep in mind," Leigh says. "There may indeed be an expert in the room who knows more about the topic, but maybe they can't speak as well as you or maybe they don't know how to smile and be light or whatever. You are up there for a reason. Someone picked you and asked you to be there because they thought you could do it."

Actor Jeremy Piven reminds himself that he's becoming fearful of what his mind believes is a bad thing. "I don't have to give in to this," he says. Jeremy compares the process to meditating. You start thinking, and you panic. You worry that you'll never be able to meditate, that your mind's too busy. Or you say, "Oh look at that thought. That's a nice thought. I'll just tuck that away for a moment."

For my friend, Dr. Sol, confidence in his capability is the difference between life and death. Surgery is actually his comfort zone. "I turn on my own music. It's like working in your garage."

But, when there's a problem, everything changes. Anxiety kicks in, and so do the questions: Is he going to lose the patient? Is this a life-threatening complication? Are people watching him? How is he going to get out of this?

Dr. Sol calms himself by moving through the process step-by-step. "It's what I call compartmentalizing. You've got to step out of the big picture, because the big picture is overwhelming. You focus on the one nail that you have to knock in. This compartmentalization is what we all need to do in order to move through anxious situations."

Dr. Sol has confidence that if he and his colleagues compartmentalize, the sequence of events will lead to a desired outcome. He recalls one case specifically: resecting a tumor in the retroperitoneal (the back of the abdomen).

"It's a large sarcoma. And the sarcoma involved the large blood vessel, the aorta. And so you had to clamp the aorta above and below the tumor and that means there's no blood flow in the heart. We're shutting off circulation. We lower the patient's body temperature to 70 degrees. Now, the person is dead, for all intents and purposes. When we're finished, we open up the blood vessels and the blood starts to clot. That means there's a clot going to the heart and from the heart to the brain and the lungs. We need to stop the clot. We open up the heart, and we literally stick our fingers in the heart to catch the clot as it's moving up."

Their hearts are racing. Their blood pressures are way up. But they can't allow themselves to get overwhelmed with the fear and anxiety associated with losing a patient. Instead, they focus only on stopping the clot.

"Did you lose the patient?" I asked.

He chuckled. "Nah. He went home."

Firefighter Billy Hayes also talks about compartmentalizing. "You learn the ability to compartmentalize your fears. It's something that's always there, but you are so focused on the goal that you can tuck it away for later. You're aware of this but you're able to focus and push through, because the more fires you go to, the better you become at your craft."

ACTION STEP:
RELIVE YOUR CONFIDENT MOMENTS

Mission
Recall a time when you felt confident. Where were you? Remember the sounds, the smells and the feeling of the space. Repeat three times.

Chapter 16: Rehearse Like a Rock Star

Fred Gretsch started by setting a goal—to buy and revive his great-great-grandfather's bankrupt company. It took him 17 years to accomplish, but he did it by using a philosophy that hits the very foundation of capability: "All achievement rests on the mastery of fundamental skills." Fred is now the president of U.S. musical instrument maker The Gretsch Company.

I've always loved Gretsch drums, but in the late 1980s, the company had very little market share, inconsistent product quality and an atrophying image. The successful turnaround began with Fred's purchase and continued with new branding concepts, modernized and expanded product design, progressive marketing and revamped distribution.

Fred doesn't actually play any of the instruments that his company makes, though, and has had an interesting time communicating with an industry of drummers, guitar players and music business people. Fred says musicians always ask him what instruments he plays. Drummers assume he beats; guitar players assume he riffs.

And he still feels intimidated by the musical banter and his responsibility to communicate effectively as the president of a major musical brand, especially since he has "a bashful side."

His answer: A little pad and pen. He's always jotting down notes, especially before a speech. "I have the highest regard for the professional performers who make it look easy. I've done my homework. When I introduce a well-known musician or player, I know who the star is.

"I write my remarks down whenever I possibly can. I rewrite them, and then I practice, practice, practice. I begin with a quote that I'm comfortable with that has a lot of deep meaning. I pick my words carefully. I begin with a blast of high energy—as much as I can muster, and I work to keep the energy high during my remarks."

Fred uses music as a metaphor, since that's his business. He rewrites those notes to the point where he feels they're not a script—they're music. "The words that come out of a page are the music of my voice. The presentation I do is representing the Gretsch legacy in history on behalf of six generations. To me, the words and music are closely related."

Former Yahoo! executive Tim Sanders is a musician, too. We've actually played together, and I helped put together some gear for his home recording studio. Tim understands the performance metaphor.

"You might be saying, I'm not a performer, so I don't need to rehearse,"

Tim says. "This isn't the way to prepare yourself for success. Your life is a series of performances with an audience, in the context of circumstances. Conversations, presentations, meetings, sales pitches, writing and skilled tasks all occur, at some point, in a make-or-break, live situation."

Those of you who've created a set list know the importance of starting with just the right song to get the audience engaged, warm up the performers and set the tone for the performance. Different performers have different approaches.

P!NK starts physically training months in advance of each tour, and that's not counting the five to six weeks of full-production rehearsals we do to integrate the music into the stage show.

When we returned to Europe for the stadium tour in 2010, we traveled with a crane. At the beginning of the show, the crane would bring a 12-foot-square box over the audience to a satellite stage that extended 50 feet from of the main stage. The band played an intro that would build as the box moved into position. We worked the music into a frenzy until the bottom of the box dropped out and P!NK plunged straight down about eight stories on a single wire, with wings on her back until she stopped, suspended right above the stage. Alecia's biggest fear is sudden drops, and she wanted to push her comfort zone and present something extraordinary to her audience

That's a different approach than that of Tony Hsieh, ZDogg or Fred Gretsch, who use well-rehearsed and simple go-to stories, quotes or jokes to ease them into a presentation. Alecia does the scariest thing she can think of to make the rest of her performance seem easy.

More recently, Alecia trained for a month to shoot the video "Try." It's a combination of modern dance, prop smashing and stunt choreography. It's magnificent and unique. The whole time, Alecia is singing live.

She shocked and inspired the music industry when she recreated that music video for the 2012 American Music Awards. She told Billboard magazine: "Making this video was the most fun I've ever had in my entire career. I never wanted it to end. It's my favorite video ever."

She's willing to go to any length to bring her presentation to the highest level and surpass her previous efforts. And she knows it requires rehearsal to take a presentation from good to great. It's the act of actually practicing the presentation. You'll also want one or several dress rehearsals during which you run your presentation in complete form, employing every component including content, movement, clothing, media, audience and worst-case scenarios.

Your preparation is the foundation. Begin with a mission statement. Then create an outline. A buddy of mine, Barry Jones, an agent with the London Speakers Bureau, told me that when he's selling a speaker, he's actually selling a solution. When you're performing, presenting, communicating or pitching, you're providing a solution for your audience. Your mission statement is that solution. Your outline dictates the step-by-step process you'll go through to get that solution to your audience. Every piece of your outline should directly reflect your mission statement. As Tim Sanders puts it, "Think of the outline as the first rehearsal prior to the creation of the product you'll present."

Being prepared isn't necessarily about being comfortable. Actor Jeremy Piven likes it that way, and he puts himself in game-time situations. He finds someone who intimidates him to run lines with and chooses practice partners who make him feel awkward. It's harder to practice in front of three people than it is to perform in front of thousands. When you put yourself in tough situations beforehand, you prepare your body and mind for "the show."

To be a better speaker, I studied with acting coach Mark Travis, because I wanted to learn how to effectively entertain an audience, paying attention to the details of my vocal inflection, body movement and facial expressions. Knowing that my favorite speakers are master storytellers, I also took lessons with a professional storyteller to get her perspective on how to give my stories more effective timing, drama, arc, release and resolve.

When I practice for a speaking gig in front of a mirror, I'm my worst (or maybe best) critic. I assess every detail of my presentation, and most importantly, make immediate improvements. I allot plenty of time for the process so I can make all the adjustments necessary to create the most effective presentation. It also makes me aware of what I don't know. (There's clarity again.)

Tim Sanders also rehearses in front of a mirror. "When you make eye contact with yourself as you verbalize your message, you become comfortable with facing one of your greatest critics—you. Later, you can easily make the same eye lock-in with others and produce a powerful gaze that exudes confidence. The result is often a more receptive audience that is willing to go along with you because they feel as if you are connecting with them. Each time I have a speaking engagement, I employ this technique in my hotel room on the day of the event. I get up early enough to allow for a verbalization of my entire speech.

"The other benefit of the mirror technique is improved adaptability.

Since I've activated my subconscious mind, it can take over during the actual performance, freeing up part of my conscious mind to observe my audience's reactions and adjust the talk on the fly as needed in response to those reactions. Because I've rehearsed well, I don't need to think to remember the next point or how I should phrase something."

Don't forget the way you look either. Mark Papia of Connexity talks about the value of dressing for success. "Fashion is also an important part of feeling secure so that you can properly convey messaging during a speech, an interview or even a meeting with a handful of folks. I happen to like the way I look in blue jackets and white shirts. If you put me in a brown sport coat and a tan shirt and said, 'Go, get on that stage and before you go up on the stage, look at yourself in this mirror,' I would not have the same level of intensity that I'd have if I got on stage in a blue blazer and a white shirt."

I learned a painful lesson about preparation back in 2004, as I was entering the realm of corporate public speaking. I got a great gig. It was the type of gig I had been wanting since I entered the market the year before—a high-energy keynote performance on a big stage for an IBM conference in Las Vegas. A member of my team was running my new Dell computer, feeding the audio and video to the show director.

I was playing drums to a video montage/audio medley of songs I had put together representing the artists I'd worked with throughout my career. It's a signature performance for me; I create new montages periodically to update my presentation. It's high energy, exciting and is usually a crowd pleaser. I rehearsed the program many times and felt confident with the performance aspect. What I hadn't done was research the details of my new computer.

This particular PC had a default setting that caused it to do a virus check at 24-hour intervals. I didn't know this. At the climax of my video montage, the computer went into a virus check, which taxed the processor. The AV stopped dead.

The show must go on, so I kept playing with a big smile on my face while quickly considering my options.

I stood up behind my drum set and lifted my arms high while clicking my sticks to get the audience clapping. As they joined, the AV kicked back in, so I slid back into the performance thinking the glitch had passed. Then, it stopped again, and started, alternating in a very unmusical and un-amusing fashion. I kept on playing, breaking into an impromptu drum solo, and then ended it quickly. This was definitely not the audience or demographic for an extended drum solo.

My tech stopped the machine and restarted the computer. I jumped off the kit a bit frazzled, my adrenaline a bit pumped, and started into my verbal presentation. Later on, I seized the opportunity to weave the AV failure into my speech as an example of how we meet with unexpected circumstances or challenges and need to own them and improvise to keep our audience engaged.

The client was not happy, and it reflected back on the meeting planner who hired me. Needless to say, I now pay meticulous attention to my media and the rehearsal necessary to employ it successfully, and I work in a contingency program if things fail.

I remember when I rehearsed my first corporate speech in front of my girlfriend and her best friend at my recording studio. My friend, Jeff, operated my visual media, and I used another friend's $10,000 projector (this was before the cheap portable projectors that are available today).

I was playing drums as part of my presentation, using an oversized video screen, so I got dressed in show clothes, put on my actual wireless microphone and did a full dress. It was uncomfortable, even though they watched me with support and love. I got a wonderfully accurate barometer of what content needed changing, what media needed tweaking, what points made me the most self-conscious, how to adjust my microphone and mic pack to be comfortable, where to walk at what points, how to position myself relative to the drums and the video screen, when I became the sweatiest and where to place my towel and water. The experience was more than valuable; it was necessary to give me accurate feedback.

In his book Today We Are Rich, Tim Sanders talks about the value of doing a dress rehearsal, which he calls "staging a simulation."

"The most effective type of rehearsal is a simulation in which you perform in circumstances nearly identical to those of the live event. This starts with some research on your part. For any presentation, first gather information on the room, the lighting and AV and seating plan. Arrange to rehearse in the actual room you'll later use. Use your visual aids, just as you will live. Recruit a few volunteers to be your audience. Bring a clock so you also rehearse your timing.

"For a conversation or informal meeting, ask a co-worker to role-play with you. Brief the person on who she's playing, including her character's personality traits and what emotions she might be feeling. If your partner is willing and time permits, reverse roles so you can experience the other side of the conversation."

When I was on the Cher tours, director Doriana Sanchez had all of the dancers watch each night's performance video on the bus ride afterward. The refinement and education you get from watching your presentation is invaluable. If a picture is worth a thousand words, then a video is worth a million. Reviewing your performance gives you clarity about what capabilities you need to examine and refine.

Billy Hayes says firefighters often go back to the scene to critique their efforts. And the stage is always a lot smaller than it seemed the day before. Your perception of venue, audience and presentation will always be different in hindsight, but the more you assess, the more accurate you'll be the day of. Review your presentations whenever possible to gain clarity for future performances.

Chapter 17: Perform Your Best Worst-Case Scenario

One of my worst anxieties comes from the fact that anything could derail or distract me at any time. Since unexpected events are among the most potent means of stimulating physiological stress reactions, many performers adopt rigid preparation schedules, ordering their lives on the day of a show so that nothing is left to chance.

I think of it differently. I imagine my worst-case scenario. It releases my anxiety and allows me to laugh at myself. Build it up in your mind as something that would be insurmountable. Once you define what that is, you remove the mystery and you gain clarity about what you would do if it happened. Then, you can anticipate that possibility during rehearsals, creating specific capability for the "what ifs." Perform your worst-case scenario until you're comfortable with it.

According to Billy Hayes, the New York fire academy utilizes buildings that closely replicate NYC buildings, just so its students can prepare running into them.

Tim Sanders doesn't just prepare for a speech; he rehearses worst-case scenarios. He prepares for potential missteps, for uncooperative audiences, for really bad performances. And Tim's been in some high-pressure situations—an officers meeting at a struggling Freddie Mac, a leadership speech to Mexican anti-gang units in their bunker (it took 30 minutes to win them over).

In *Today We Are Rich*, he also gives some useful action steps. "An important part of preparation is to anticipate objections to the points you'll make in conversation or presentation. Outline answers to overcome those, and separately rehearse presenting them to your skeptical audience member or conversational partner. The more you face objections during preparation, the more you'll be convinced that you are right, which will give you conviction when it counts.

"Distractions are the hardest things to prepare for. Ringing cell phones, fire alarms, people suddenly getting up and leaving the room—all of these can fluster you, regardless of how much you've rehearsed." Rehearse dealing with these distractions, Tim says.

"When you are flying on a plane and catching up on your emails, convert the crying baby behind you from an annoyance to an opportunity to perform with distractions. When you are in a meeting or talking and a cell phone rings or someone whips out his or her BlackBerry to check email, treat it as an opportunity for you to learn to ignore it. This will not only prepare you better but also transmute distractions from negative experiences to constructive opportunities."

It's how I imagine astronauts prepare for space flight—rehearsing every possible scenario so that there is no room for mistake or miscalculation. To find out, I interviewed spaceman and former fighter pilot Alan Bean (yes, a decorated fighter pilot turned astronaut and a rock 'n' roll drummer discussing shared experiences.)

I did my homework. I knew he'd be critical of my concepts and ask questions about my background. He's conservative, analytical and about as un-rock 'n' roll as they come, and what he told me about traveling through space was far less dramatic than I anticipated. Why? Because of preparation.

The Navy knows it's scary up there, so its airmen start by flying simple aircraft and performing simple maneuvers. Once they've mastered those, they move on to more complex planes that do more dangerous exercises. The pilots learn to overcome small fears. Alan recalls one particularly harrowing training day.

"We walked out to the airplane, and the pilot said, 'This airplane has had a series of false fire warning lights, so it's possible we'll see that today. They've tried to fix it, but they haven't seemed to have found the problem.'

"We take off, and we're flying; everything is great. And all of a sudden that fire warning light comes on. I knew that a fire warning light was one of the worst things you could have in an airplane—that you might have to eject. I had a difficult time concentrating on flying that airplane, even though I knew it was probably false."

Alan recognized the value in an exercise that forced him to concentrate in spite of his anxiety. Later on in his career, he experienced things a lot more scary than fire warning lights, but they weren't nearly as traumatic, because he'd learned through vigorous practice and preparation how to stay focused on his capability when things weren't perfect.

It was the same way with NASA. Astronauts go through all sorts of game-time scenarios, so that when they're on an actual space mission, and doing all sorts of really amazing, dangerous things, they've already experienced what it's like—which is why it wasn't overwhelming for Alan to actually travel to the moon. But he does humbly admit that nothing could really have prepared him for the unearthly experience of stepping out of the ship and space walking. "I opened the door, and there was nothing—just space."

That wasn't fear though; it was awe.

Sometimes the worst-case scenario happens and it creates magical opportunities. There's a natural sense of empathy from your audience when adversity appears, especially when it deals with things that you did not anticipate and that your audience identifies as truly out of your control.

Drummer Stewart Copeland told a story about The Police's first arena gig, at Madison Square Garden in New York City. Selling out the show wasn't the problem—it was adjusting from the small stage to a massive arena with a dispersed audience, strange acoustics, a cold space...and a drummer's worst nightmare: a broken bass drum head with the beater stuck through it.

"Now, if a snare drum breaks, you can pull it and throw in another one in a heartbeat. No one even notices. If a tom-tom breaks, you flip it over, no problem. But if the bass drum breaks, you've got to pull out all the mics and cymbal stands and all the drums to get to the thing. You have to stop the show."

And they did. "Sting stepped up to the microphone and started telling jokes and singing songs, and the other crew came out like a Chinese fire drill, clowning around. By the time they got that kit stripped down, the skin put on that drum and the whole rig rebuilt, the audience was in a frenzy of anticipation.

"'OK. Are we all ready? We're all right. Two, three, four.' The place exploded. Now, we owned New York City, and it was that little moment of adversity that made it happen. The worst had happened, and we were over that now."

The audience sensed it wasn't supposed to happen like that. It was unique. They were there the night something special happened. "The little off-the-script repartee—Sting learned that craft on a cruise liner, by the way, where he learned how hit songs were constructed—that was the icebreaker."

Copeland learned an early lesson: The worst thing can be a blessing. You can turn it to your advantage in a way that takes the hex off your need to be perfect. It can be real instead. Zappos CEO Tony Hsieh has reduced it to a simple worst-case scenario. "Like 10,000 to 20,000 years ago, the worst-case scenario was you get eaten by a saber-toothed tiger. Now, the worst-case scenario is you might have to crash on a friend's couch."

And there are those who invite difficulty, who actually use it to advance their presentation. Take it from the adversity maven Dr. Paul Stoltz.

"Adversity can be so great. Your audience recognizes it and thinks, 'Whoa, this dude's the real deal' and [something going wrong] was a great demonstration of exactly what he's talking about." Paul looks for it. He embraces it. He craves those moments when things screw up, because it gives him accelerated credibility and energy.

He approaches every gig with a bring-it-on mindset. "I dare ya! Bring it on!"

Mark Papia says there are degrees of failure in the boardroom—tactical failures, which can be brushed off, and strategic failures, which are much harder to handle—failures to your credibility or your brand that could be game changing.

"Say you go in unprepared. You give a crappy presentation. The client says no. There are other issues, like the client thinking, 'Wow, I can't believe how unprepared he was. That type of person would never work here.' So, one 'no' can easily become 10 'nos.' And then they think, 'I will never take another meeting with that person. I will not be a reference for that person.' These really are degrees of failure," Mark says.

"Most people who put in the prep time are free from the fear of the strategic failure. I mean what is the worst thing that can happen? 'I'm prepared. My content is rich and compelling. I might be off, you know. They might think I'm a seven when it comes to presenting and not a nine if I'm off.' As long as a person does the advance work, puts in the prep time and shows up with a clear head ready to present, I'm down with the 'what's the worst that can happen?' Because there's not a lot of bad that could come from that.

"Let's say that you're standing in front of a conference room with 30 people, you present and you don't wow them—your presentation may be missing an element. Somebody will still raise their hand and say, 'Hey, I like the presentation, and I like where you're going, but an important part of our business is X, Y and Z. How might your proposal or your presentation change to account for that?' So, in a sense what you got was a 'no,' but now you've got more information that will enable you to tailor it to a 'yes.' You might be able to do that on the fly. It might require a second meeting. It might require you doing some developmental work."

There are tactical components to every presentation that you just can't control.

"If you look at the presentation side of it, you're in front of a thousand people and you're presenting an idea. Twenty percent of the people in the audience are not going to agree with what you have to say, anyway. If you're speaking from the heart, if you're speaking with conviction, if it's obvious that you're buttoned up and you know your stuff, people may say, 'Well, the guy is a dope for his logic, but it was a good a presentation. He clearly laid out his arguments, and it was easy to follow.' When you're dealing with a room of a thousand people, you would expect dysfunction anyway so you just have to be prepared."

Strategic failure closes the door to future business. With a tactical failure, the answer could be 'no,' but there is an open door for other opportunities. As Mark says: "People say no to me all the time. And every time somebody says no to me, I'm somewhat excited knowing that I'm one 'no' closer to a 'yes.'"

ACTION STEP:
DEFINE YOUR WORST-CASE SCENARIO

Mission

Think about an intimidating presentation and identify the worst thing that could happen. Then, determine what you would do next. Repeat this until you laugh. The laugh represents release. With every release comes a realization, or moment of clarity, that enables you to think about logical choices and actions. Create a plan so you feel secure with your contingency should your worst-case scenario actually occur.

Chapter 18: Give Us a Smile

Guitarist Steve Stevens makes it simple, but very effective.

"I can't tell you how many bands or musicians I've seen, and they may be playing well or they may be playing songs that I like, but they look like they're not having fun. By showing people that you're enjoying what you do, you win. You can't help but win people over by smiling. You disarm them. Even if you make a mistake, or you're nervous, people are willing to overlook it. They want you to be good, and they'll do what they need to do to help you get your show on. Smile: It shows that you're happy and grateful to be there."

I have used smiling as a quick way to get over my nerves. I've even experimented with audiences. I've asked everyone to give me big fake smiles and keep them there for at least 15 seconds. The smile becomes authentic, even on the skeptics.

Smiling has other benefits, too. It makes you more attractive, which can increase your confidence. It exercises the muscles in your face; it's an immediate facelift that makes you look younger.

It can shift the mood. There's a chemical reaction that occurs in the body when you smile that releases endorphins and serotonin. Endorphins are your own private narcotic. They are neurotransmitters (chemicals that pass along signals from one neuron to the next), opiate-like chemicals that produce feelings of euphoria and calmness in response to stress, fear or pain. They interact mainly with receptors in cells found in regions of the brain responsible for blocking pain and controlling emotion. Serotonin is also a neurotransmitter directly affecting mood, sleep patterns and appetite.

Smiling gives you a natural high that can relieve performance anxiety. It can also reduce your blood pressure and boost your immune system. I recall a neurosurgeon at a party talking about facial expressions that singers make. He said that there are endorphin, serotonin and dopamine releases in the brain when opera singers make an "O" shape with their mouths, and it feels really good to do it.

ACTION STEP:
SMILE!

Mission

Smile. Hold it for at least 15 seconds. Note how it makes you feel. Set your alarm on your mobile phone to three random times during the day. When the alarm goes off, smile. Observe how it makes you feel, and how it affects people around you. Share the experience with others. The next time you feel any kind of anxiety, smile! Pick certain moments in your presentation where you have a prepared smile. If it's appropriate, share it with your audience.

Chapter 19: Get the Gig

Marc Cenedella is responsible for the gainful employment of many people. He's spent the last seven years as founder of one of the hottest job sites out of New York City, TheLadders.com, and most recently co-authored the bestselling book, *You're Better Than Your Job Search*. He's also the consummate expert on helping people deal with arguably one of the highest anxiety performances on the planet—the job interview. Here are his tips to overcoming the anxiety of that particular performace. Notice how all of them herald back to capability—and practice.

1. **Show up with a "good" level of knowledge after doing a "reasonable" amount of research.** You'd be surprised at the number of people who haven't looked at the company's homepage, Googled its name and checked out the stockticker before showing up for an interview. Likewise, you might be surprised at the number of people who overdo it and show up with eight pages of questions— single-spaced—and start off with an inquiry as to why margins in the Southwest region have declined by 10 percent in the past seven years despite favorable currency rates.

2. **Be on time and unflustered, with a clean, well-presented copy of your résumé.** Sure, this sounds like "Interviewing 101," but you know you've violated this rule at least once in your life because you didn't leave the house 10 minutes earlier than you thought was safe. Do yourself a favor—it's far better to waste 10 minutes in the lobby than stressing out in transit.

3. **Dress the part—businesslike and professional, no matter how groovy the company is.** Except in cases where the culture is aggressively anti-corporate, a coat-and-tie or demure pearls never make you look bad.

4. **Be kind to every employee you meet**. As a matter of fact, be kind to everybody within two miles of the building—the receptionist, the parking lot guy, the janitor and the intern. When I ask our receptionists how a candidate behaved, it's shocking to hear the number of people who think good manners and kindness are only to be trotted out in the interview room.

5. **Remember JFK.** Or remember what your parents told you about JFK. Ask not what the company can do for you, answer instead what you can do for this company.

6. **This isn't *Real Housewives*.** It's a job interview in which you will explain and sell your ability to do a job. Stick to business and how you can solve the problems your future boss is facing. Don't go into a half-hour long disquisition on the relative merits of Mozart and Beethoven, the reasons you love or hate the Yankees or the intricacies of your college rivalries. The interviewer does not want your life story, he or she wants to know your business capabilities.

7. **"Bad mouth thee, bad mouth me."** When you trash-talk your former or current employer, guess what the interviewer thinks? "If we hire this guy, I'm next on the firing line!" Never, ever say bad, mean, unkind or even unflattering true things if it displays your ability to be an ingrate, gossip or ne'er-do-well.

8. **Save the money talk for last.** You should get a range from the recruiter or HR director before going in ("in the interests of saving everybody time, I need to know what range this position is budgeted for") and side-step the grilling about your current compensation ("my understanding is that we're talking about a future position at your company and what my skills and talents would be worth in that regard, not what I've been paid in the past for a different role, with different responsibilities, at a different company—am I correct in assuming that or am I off-base?"). Don't bring it up in interviews until after they know how excited they are about working with you, because that's when they're most likely to get excited about paying you more.

9. **Thank the interviewer for his or her time and ask a few good questions.** The best one: How can I help you get a gold star on your review next year? A great all-purpose question: "Is there anything else I should have asked about this role or my future boss that I haven't asked already?"

10. **Send a thank you email.** Thank the interviewer again and reiterate, briefly, what you discussed and how you can contribute. Three sentences is a good length—five sentences maximum. For example: "I enjoyed our conversation about the changes in the mobile ecosystem and how my background will be useful in designing the advertising strategy for the Big Mick in McDowell's upcoming national campaign." This helps the interviewer remember why they like you when time comes to make the go/no-go decision on hiring you.

But Marc's not perfect. He wrote about his personal experience with a bombed interview and his subsequent insights online in an essay he has graciously allowed me to include herein. As you read it, think about capability and preparation as they relate to the interview process.

Boy, I Blew That Interview

I was coming out of business school, and had scored a great interview opportunity with a top investment firm in New York. I'd had a few great rounds with the team, but that day I was meeting with the "name" partners—the big guns who had founded the firm and whose names were on the door.

The senior partner was kind of an imperious fellow and, frankly speaking, not my cup of tea. But that was OK, because everybody else I'd met had an energy and an entrepreneurial drive that seemed well-suited to me. I was psyched.

But I just wasn't clicking with this guy, and then he dropped my least favorite interview question of all time. It's the question that they teach you not to ask in Interviewing 101 because it is so obvious, and so easily manipulated by the interviewee. It was that old hoary chestnut: "What's your greatest weakness?"

"Brevity."

And, not saying another word, stared politely right back at him. Probably with a little bit of a wise-ass grin. OK, it was a pretty juvenile response, and I let my capricious side get the better of me.

Needless to say, things went downhill from there, and the interview ended in a polite, "don't-let-the-door-hit-you-on-the-way-out" manner a few minutes later. Man, I blew that interview. And I felt like a schmuck.

So, it's inevitable that, some days, in some places, you'll really goof up an interview. And we've all blown interviews before. A job interview is artificial and awkward. You can feel like a butterfly under the magnifying glass, and it is uncomfortable to have somebody else poking and prodding you. And it is how we handle the recovery that makes us great professionals.

Follow through with dignity. You're probably feeling sheepish and a bit embarrassed, and would prefer to just hide your head in the sand. But as a $100K+ professional, that's not what you're going to do. Look, the best way of overcoming the failed job interview is to show those people who witnessed your setback that you are made of sterner stuff.

Write polite, but brief, thank-you notes and be gracious. There's no sense whatsoever in trying to overcome your gaffe, so don't address it. Just thank them for their time, and let them know how much you enjoyed the opportunity. You'll feel like you've come out a little bit ahead, and your interviewers will feel like your show of class is impressive.

Blow off steam. Go for a run, take a hike, jump into the lap pool. However you get your exercise, a little physical activity will take your mind off it, and let you get the stress out of your system.

Move on. If you've really blown the interview, there is no sense in wasting more time on it. You've got better things to do. The mark of a champion is to put the loss behind you and concentrate on doing better next time.

(And a brief word to the wise, you really need to separate your emotions about the interview process from your rational assessment of your performance. I can't tell you how many hires we've made here at TheLadders who later confided to me that they thought they had done poorly in the interviews. It is natural to feel anxious about the interview, but don't let that fool you into thinking you've actually, really and truly blown the interview.)

Get better. What was it that tripped you up? Knowledge about the company? Insight into that new technology? A few questions about an area that you hadn't really thought about in the past few years? Whatever it was, use this as an opportunity to bone up for future interviews. Never see failure as failure—it's just a chance to get better for the next time.

Chapter 20: Fake It 'Til You Make It

Try this tip from Ronda Beaman, a professor of leadership and speech for California Polytechnic University and the author of a delightful book called *Little Miss Merit Badge*: Believe that you'll help just one person become bigger, better or more than they ever thought they could be.

"It's about helping other people. There are only so many ways that I can help other people, and this seems to be the one I'm best at—sharing my stories, my beliefs and the largeness and greatness of the human condition. If it's about me, then I'm going to be rendered paralyzed by fear. If it's about helping or enlightening or empowering someone else, then I can do it."

Also, act confident.

"I grew up wanting to be an actress, but I didn't have the self-esteem and probably didn't have the talent. It wasn't my real calling, or I would have been one. So, now I act like I'm confident. I come into a room where all my clients are or I enter a classroom of 200 kids and for the first five minutes I'm acting the part. I act like I've been hired along with the best script writer, the best director, the best lighting and costumes, and my role is giving this speech. And after about five minutes, I have the role. I feel good."

It's that old saying: Fake it until you make it. Fake confidence until you have it.

But five minutes can feel like an eternity if you're overwhelmed with anxiety or fear. I've had the fear of being an imposter, had dreams of being discovered as a fraud. Dr. Valerie Young writes about impostor syndrome: "You may feel like a fraud but in truth your fear of being inadequate pales in comparison to your fear of being extraordinary." Despite external evidence of competence, people with this syndrome are convinced that they are frauds and that they don't deserve the success they've achieved.

Truthfully, if you're being of service, who cares? Take all that energy and put it into your audience. For the sake of being cheeky, even if you are an imposter, if you promote the wellbeing of others, does it matter? That's why being audience-centric is so powerful; it makes all these internal noises and considerations so inconsequential.

Even if you feel like you're acting the part, we're not talking about false confidence here. Ronda's insights are based on the fact that you've done the work and you really do have something to say or do. I have frequently performed for at-risk kids in detention camps. They're filled with fear and anger—and certainly disregard for an "old" rocker like me. But you know what? If I can reach one kid (and I know I'm gonna reach one kid), and if that kid's life is changed by what I say, I've done my job.

Ronda says that's all she wants. "If you can be part of that, it can help you overcome an awful lot of your own failings and fears. Once you help other people, whether it's volunteering, teaching, performing music, acting—whatever it is—and you're doing it for the enjoyment and benefit of others, you get it back threefold."

People appreciate authentic willingness, she says. She tells her students that people are much kinder than we give them credit for.

Tony Hsieh's biggest tip: Start with a go-to story, something guaranteed to touch the audience or get laughs. He always has confidence in that story. "For those first two or three minutes, when your voice is shaky and heart is pounding, you're basically on autopilot. It gets out of your system, because you know the audience always responds.

Jobs maven Marc Cenedella actually gets pretty nervous before a presentation—who knew? At first he looked for ways to effectively distract himself, but his current technique brings much more to his presentation—audience participation.

Getting the audience involved distracts him, and makes him feel like it's on his side. He prepares several questions he can ask. Onstage, he says: "Hey everybody, I know this is a big issue. [Pause.] Wait. Maybe it's not a big issue. How many people have found that technology has made recruiting easier for you? OK, that's about 80 percent of your hands. How many people have found that it's actually made it tougher? OK, about 20 percent."

He's not only learned something key about his audience, he now feels like they're all in it together.

Marc's final words of wisdom: "Remember, you're not the first person to have stage fright. You're the billionth person to have stage fright." He also brought up the popular quote from beatnik, music manger and author James Neil Hollingworth, who wrote under the pseudonym Ambrose Redmoon, "Courage is not the absence of fear, but rather the judgment that something else is more important than fear."

Chapter 21: Use Your Ego

Ultimately, you have to have confidence in your preparation. For this, I'll use a story from Ray Parker Jr., who started his career as a first-call studio guitar master and songwriter working with the likes of Aretha Franklin, Chaka Khan, Gladys Knight, Diana Ross and Tina Turner before he hit it big as an aritist with the Ghostbusters theme song and a subsequent stream of hits.

Ray's first professional gig was with The Spinners when he was 13 years old. The group's founder, Billy Henderson, gave little Ray the complex chart for "Fascinating Rhythm" by George Gershwin.

"He looked at me and said, 'If you can read this, we'll take you on tour'— even though they were only gonna play 'It's a Shame' or some straight song. That's how he decided that you were a real musician. I was young. I'd never been on a concert stage before with real Motown acts."

He read the chart, and one of the musicians, G. C. Cameron showed him the ropes on the tour. "Luckily for me, I wasn't at the front of the stage, I was in the background. But it felt like the spotlight was on me."

Ever since, conquering stage fright has all been in his head. "I've always been an egomaniac—in a positive sense, though, not an offensive egomaniac god. A lot of people think, 'Oh crap! What if something bad happens?' I've usually thought, 'Well, what if I win?'

"A lot of times in life, you're going to make some money, and you're gonna lose some. Let's say you made $100,000, and then you messed up and you only have $50,000 left. Is the glass half empty or is it half full? Are you looking at the $50,000 you lost? Or are you gonna look at the $50,000 that you're ahead?

It's similar to what rock star guitar player and my friend, Steve Stevens, thinks. He admits that the way he looks onstage has nothing to do with how he feels inside.

His advice: "Be totally prepared with whatever it is you're going to do. I don't ever want to get on stage and think, 'Do I really know the songs?'"

Preparation eliminates the toxicity of doubt. "Once you doubt yourself, all the negative emotions come into play. So, if you're going to do a presentation or you're going to play songs with your band, make sure you're prepared. Then, let your ego kick in."

But Steve is opposed to setting up false confidence, especially if you don't have the goods to back it up. "Ego has never made an OK performance into a great performance. There are a lot of times you've seen performers who are all ego and," he laughed, "have nothing to back it up with. If you're really prepared, you can be the best that you have the potential to be. 'I'm going to play the best solo I can play. I'm going to get the best sound together.' You can concentrate on all these things, because you know that you've got your foundation."

Steve remembers being brought in to work on The Assassins with Sylvester Stallone and Antonio Banderas. "Mark Mancina [Con Air] was the composer, and he knew I could play flamenco guitar. What he didn't know: I don't read music, or I can't read it very well. I sat down and got out my guitar. But when I saw the sheet music, I got really scared. I tried to bluff it, and I was failing miserably."

Steve finally just asked to speak to Mancina, and told him that he probably wasn't the best guy for job. "'But if you wanna give me a shot, play me the music and let me interpret it in my own way. Let me play what I think would be appropriate, and I won't take more than 15 or 20 minutes of your time.' It ended up working well, and he appreciated my honesty."

Never be afraid of preparing by reaching out for input. Steve co-wrote many hit songs with Billy Idol and is musical director of his band. "Our rhythm guitar player, Billy Morrison, is a total punk-rock guitar player. What I love about him is he's the first to say, 'I can't play anything like you can.' But the guy will work really hard and be honest with me. Don't make excuses, just be honest, because if you're lying to me, I'm never going to know what you actually know."

Be brutally honest with yourself. Assess where you stand in your research and education (clarity) and your preparation (capability) so that your expectations are aligned with your skill set. World-class performers don't kid themselves. They're also willing to go to extremes to get an edge.

Steve remembers when a set list for all-star cover band Rock 'N' Roll Allstars included three Def Leppard songs. "Those guitar parts are really complicated. So, I went right to the source. I sent an email to lead vocalist Joe Elliot and I said, 'Do you by any chance have the multi-tracks [of the original recorded guitar parts] or something where I can hear exactly what's going on?' Joe not only found the separate versions, he gladly sent them on."

Chapter 22: Hit the Stage

No matter how much preparation you do, you can still only gain true refinement—and the resulting confidence—from hours spent in the ring, at the podium, in the conference room, on the band stand or fighting the fire.

Look at The Beatles. They started playing together seven years before landing in the U.S.—a good band from Liverpool that became great by clocking thousands of performance hours playing in Hamburg between 1960 and 1962. In Outliers, Malcolm Gladwell writes that The Beatles spent 270 nights playing for between five and eight hours per night. By the time they had their seminal success in 1964, they had played nearly 1,200 times. About the Hamburg experience, John Lennon once said, "We got better and got more confident. We couldn't help it with all the experience playing all night long. It was handy them being foreign. We had to try even harder, put our hearts and souls into it, to get ourselves over."[7]

Firefighter Billy Hayes did the same.

"I had an extensive background in that familiar environment through all the training, but until I actually went into a burning building for the first time, I didn't 100 percent know how I was going to react. Then, you get to the point of experience where you can do it without even realizing what you're doing and respect the fact that it becomes like muscle memory."

Leigh Gallagher of *FORTUNE* (the TV/radio commentator) talks about her initial experiences on air, when she worked at *Forbes Magazine* and was chosen for the weekly show *Forbes On Fox*.

"I discovered that the only way to get better in television was to just keep getting back on the horse again when you feel like you've fallen off. You just get back on it. The path to getting better is the experience. I had the opportunity to do this show and that helped me make the transition [on air] much more easily, although it took a long time."

When Ray Parker Jr. took on the role of front man, fear kicked in. Although he had his 10,000 performance hours as a guitar player, his new gig required an additional skill set.

"I knew I couldn't sing that well. There're 5,000 or 6,000 people out there, and I gotta sing front and center? The microphone and the spotlight are on me; it ain't on someone else. I'm not standing in the back anymore with the

---

[7] From the book, *Shout!* by Philip Norman

drummer." (No offense taken, Ray!)

He'd been on stage thousands of times, but never like that, with the whole show depending on him. "That was a pretty scary time." So, he told the sound guy to turn the backgrounds and guitar up and his lead vocals the heck down.

"I know I looked pretty. You know, I got my hair done, and my clothes happening. I'm gonna rock with the guitar, and the girls are gonna be happy. Just make sure they hear a little bit of what I'm saying, and let's get on with it."

It actually took Ray a couple of years before he developed the confidence to sing comfortably on stage, and those two years were filled with an awful lot of practice on stage. There are distinct capabilities that a performer, presenter or communicator can only gain from actual presentation.

Foreigner lead singer Kelly Hansen remembers opening up for Led Zeppelin at the O2 arena in London. The charity show had been postponed because Jimmy Page fractured a finger, which changed the plans for all of the performers involved.

"It was so chaotic. We had to change our tour plans to make the date. We went straight to a sound check where Bill Wyman [of The Rolling Stones] was directing people. There were cables everywhere. That whole day, you're meeting people. You're shuffling around. You're seeing everybody in the world, from Paul McCartney to whomever else, and there are people coming in and out of the dressing room.

"It's like skydiving. You know the plane won't fly around forever. You have to jump out. After a few times, you start getting used to it. I don't think the feeling of uneasiness or nervousness ever completely goes away, but you start getting more accustomed to the experience. And you need to trust the people handling the organization of your production and your sound system and your monitoring. Then, you can feel much more relaxed about going out."

NFL sideline reporter Laura Okmin spent weeks prepping for her interview with quarterback Vince Young. She was planning to ask him about some very personal information. His response would determine how she would navigate the rest of the interview. "We sat down at his kitchen table. He'd just had his first son. He said something about the baby and about not sleeping. I knew about his past from all the preparation and study I'd done. I just sort of just zeroed in, 'You didn't have much of a childhood, did you?'"

And he opened up, telling Laura about his childhood nickname: Crack Baby. He described how his mother used to deal with him. She'd lock him in his bedroom, and he'd look out through a peephole and watch her and her friends doing drugs and having sex, until she made him go outside, where he got his ass kicked every night for being Crack Baby.

"All of a sudden, we start talking about his time in Tennessee, the beginning of his fall with the Titans. Luckily, I knew enough about him to be able to go into another place. I asked, 'OK, so at what point when you were booed two years ago, did you start hearing Crack Baby in your head?' And he said, 'Immediately.'"

SECTION 3: CONFIDENCE

"Action is a great restorer and builder of confidence. Inaction is not only the result, but also the cause of fear. Perhaps the action you take will be successful; perhaps different action or adjustments will have to follow. But any action is better than no action at all."

—Norman Vincent Peale

People who fight for a living fascinate me, particularly mixed martial artists, because their sport is so brutal. What could possibly rattle their nerves? Fighter Kendall Grove told me he once almost drowned in the ocean—but that pales in comparison to some of his moments in the octagon.

His first amateur fight qualifies, against the also-debuting Marvelous Tefaga. He remembers every moment: the smell of the wood on the platform, the thickness and smell (like kerosene) of the ropes, the paint on the canvas ("like claws, like a real boxing ring").

The whole time, he was thinking of every possible outcome, every possible way he could get his butt kicked and every possible way he could really kick some butt (clarity). He did so much preparation that he was emotionally exhausted before he even fought (capability).

"The one thing I know I was repeating in my head: 'I can't lose. I can't lose. I can't lose. I can't lose. I just came back from Vegas. I was training out there with Marc Laimon, John Lewis and Phil Baroni. Phil told me I should become a pro fighter, and I'm doing it. OK, I can't lose. I can't lose. I can't lose! I want to do this for the rest of my life. I've got to win this fight.'"

He knew he was good—nah, he knew he was great. So, he tapped into the confidence he had in his preparation for the fight. And that confidence brought him success.

"You've got everything resting on it; you can't not master it. Even though it's your first time, you've got to do it. It's not safe. You put in all the time and energy as a professional, not just a mixed martial artist, but as a professional to be on that level. You put in your hours, your dedication, your blood, sweat and tears. At that point, you've invested so much, there's no backing out."

Even today, a decade or more in, Kendall still gets performance anxiety. He describes the angel on one shoulder, the devil on the other.

Devil G: "Am I really supposed to be fighting?"

Angel G: "I was born to do this."

Devil G: "Wait a minute. Wait a minute! This guy's good."

Angel G: "You're good, too. Look who you beat."

Then the fighter steps in. Knowing you've clocked the hours and done it many times before sets the natural foundation for confidence.

If you have clarity, it's easier to become capable. With capability comes confidence—real confidence. (Beware of the false kind, the confidence you see on reality show competitions, from the man with a voice that would scare a family of raccoons.) It's based on an unclear assessment of actual capability.

Real confidence is the result of real capability, which always comes from the simple and true clarification of a goal and the diligent development of skill.

I've simplified this process to allow a smaller margin of error. It's useful, regardless of your individual goals. There is no substitute for real confidence.

Chapter 23: Some Pre-performance Rituals

MC Fong Sai U of The Roots always closed his eyes on stage, and he didn't open them until the performance was over. He was so nervous that he never saw the crowd.

"The first time I opened my eyes, man, it was a different experience. I caught that rush for the first time 'cause I got to see the crowd rockin', and then I got to see the reactions to certain words. After that, the whole mission is to keep my eyes open."

Today, Fong Sai U has two pre-performance rituals. The first: Silence. "I don't like anybody to talk to me before I go on stage. I don't like any of that. Like, I just want to be in my zone. My mind is blank."

The second: Competition. Instead of focusing on his performance, he focuses on the performances of his peers, i.e., his challengers.

"This is a competitive sport, being the emcee. I'm concentrating on the person who's up there now. I'm seeing what you do, to see how, when I come on stage, I'm going to destroy what you just did. We're dueling our mics."

He changes his mindset. When nervousness starts to overtake him, he consciously makes a shift to put his attention on aggressive competition. It's become almost a Pavlovian response now that he has done it so many times. This is similar to what athletes do—associating adrenaline with boosting their performance. Fong Sai U now links that rush with competition. "I'm just gonna think competitive thoughts instead of being nervous. I'm gonna rip his head off instead of being nervous."

Some like it quiet; some like it loud. Guitarist Steve Stevens listens to the music that inspired him as a kid. "I'm still that kid that went to see Led Zeppelin. Remind yourself of that, and be grateful that you're somebody people are going to pay money to come see. You're drawing on the spirits of your influencers—for me, Miles Davis or King Crimson. You're using it to bolster yourself and give yourself confidence, because you realize that you are now that inspiration to somebody else."

And it is not just musical performers who like it loud to get into the zone of success. In an episode of TV show *The Office*, Dwight Schrute listened to Metallica before a big sales pitch to enhance his mood. Want some real life examples? Billion-dollar salesman Mark Papia of Connexity uses music to shift his mood, too.

"If I have to give a presentation at 10 a.m., and somebody makes me mad at 8 a.m., I'm not going to be in the right frame of mind to give a fun, energetic presentation. If I need a pick me up, in the car going to the speech, I throw in a Led Zeppelin playlist. I'm not talking 'Stairway to Heaven.' 'Whole Lotta Love' would pick me up. 'Black Dog' would pick me up. 'Rock and Roll' would pick me up.

"The same thing holds true with job interviews, if you're only going to chat with one person. I would argue that a job interview is actually more stressful than a presentation to 1,000 people. If you're going to a job interview at 10 a.m., and your wife just threw you a curve ball and you're in that funk, music can also get you out. You're going to be up a notch and feeling good and more comfortable and you're not going to be self-conscious about being a downer."

Leigh Gallagher of *FORTUNE* talks about her transition from print to broadcast media. "People that work in print journalism are not usually known for being particularly television ready. That 'sloppy journalist' stereotype exists for a reason. But if you feel like you look good, then it makes it a lot more fun."

People don't "hear" you on TV; they "see" you on TV. "Television is a crazy animal that way. Live speaking is a little different, but they're both about being comfortable."

If you're comfortable in your environment, in your own skin and clothes, people know it—but they know the opposite as well. Your body language reflects it. Do not underestimate the value of making sure you feel like you look good because the confidence it brings is real.

I know few people who are as conscientious about their visual appearance (and the confidence it inspires) as Cher. One is the longtime director of Cher's iconic live shows, Doriana Sanchez. She still recalls her anxieties back in 1999 when we began rehearsing for Cher's *Believe* tour.

"There's a learning curve, and a lot of it has to do with human safety in the air. We had to be really, really, really careful, and I remember questioning a thousand times over and over, 'Am I doing the right thing? Am I safe enough? What are the backups?' There was so much preparation and so much rehearsal involved in pulling these things off."

So, Dori created a sacred place in her hotel room. When she was working in Las Vegas, a city full of energy, she meditated in the walk-in closet on pillows next to her shoes and clothes.

"I'd sit on the floor, and do my meditation and prayer work before going into rehearsal, and keep myself really cloaked in prayer and in mindfulness. That's what allows me to be the calm in the center of the storm. Then, when I go and deal with an artist, I can come to them from a place of peace rather than chaos, because the chaos is already spinning around us. It's important that my being is in peace and that I can convey that to the artist so they don't have so much fear."

Dori also knows the importance of being playful at work—something she learned during her gig as dancer/choreographer for the movie *Dirty Dancing*. She didn't know what the movie would become, but she knew it was going to be fun.

"I had worked with the choreographer, but there was no guarantee that I was going to get it. In the end, I just decided to have fun and not worry about the outcome. That's been my thing ever since then—have fun, even when it's a pressure situation. Because, in the end, that's really what it is all about. Then, other people will come on your happy train."

That's what she tells the young performers on *So You Think You Can Dance*. "They're at the beginning of their careers, and they're so panicked and exhausted, all I can tell them is just enjoy. Have fun. And that seems to be my thing—to help people have fun—because in the end, that's what we do. We're here to create joy.

"When I was taking an acting class, years ago, the acting coach would prepare us for auditions. He would make us clap and scream and do all this crazy stuff in a corner, and then go right into our scene work. It brought us to a higher state of energy by shaking out all our scary little monsters."

Dori also has a strong belief in what she calls mirror work. Her philosophy is, "We are perfect, whole and complete and we are well equipped to do whatever we need to do in that moment. We have to know that and allow our magnificence to come through. Look in the mirror, and say, 'I am magnificent, perfect, whole and complete,' again and again. Take deep breaths in and out while continuing the eye contact. The breath is revitalizing, rejuvenating."

These processes have inspired Dori and many other stage performers over the years. But athletes such as surfer Garrett McNamara use them, too.

"When I was a kid, people always told me how they got butterflies, and I never got them. I didn't really understand it. As I got older, I started surfing giant waves, and I'd get the rush, especially when I was on a ride that had a 50/50 chance of making the wave. The fear factor finally started kicking in, telling me that if I didn't make it, I could get hurt. I could die. And I'd get a rush from that fear. But, as I surfed these waves over and over, I got desensitized."

Then, in 2002, he met Jaws at the Tow-in Surfing World Cup. Jaws is the nickname for Pe'ahi, a surf break on Maui's north shore. Garrett says, at the time, it was the "gnarliest, biggest, most frightening place" he'd ever been. The first wave of the contest, he recalls "wussing out."

So, he started talking to himself, reminding himself about his past successes, building his confidence based on his actual past performances, all the hours of mastering his craft and how much that really did mean at this very moment. This helped him build confidence. Garrett had the skill set, but this was the first time that he had to really work to create the mindset. It was a defining moment, and it worked. He and tow-in partner Rodrigo Resende won top prize.

That was Garrett's first real experience with fear. It freaked him out, and it inspired him to take a deeper look at himself and his purpose and start thinking about things differently. "I was thinking about what could happen; I wasn't in the moment."

The next year, he returned to Jaws, and caught a wave with a 20-foot barrel. Onlookers thought the lip crushed him. He remembers the wave with clarity. "I saw myself doing it. I was in the moment. I stayed in the moment. It was one of my most amazing rides. I didn't get the fear rush, and I had an enlightening experience. Things just went silent."

But like masters of any craft, Garrett wanted more. He journeyed up to Alaska to surf under 300-foot-tall glaciers. "We were sitting so close death. It was the most horrifying, fearful experience I've ever had, and I wanted to leave right after my first wave."

Something had shifted in him. "It didn't seem worth it—the rush. It wasn't worth it to be so close to death for that ride. From that day on, I didn't get the rush anymore in the barrel. No matter where I surfed, no matter how big."

So, he started doing research, studying and reading books and learning about "how things are and why and what everything is about." His mentor, Kent Ewing, introduced him to the concept of being present, connected and protected. If you're present, you're connected to what's going on; you're protected.

Garrett employs two breathing techniques. The first one he calls "purging," which uses belly breaths (if you've had vocal training, you may know this as diaphragm breathing). He extends his belly out as air comes in for two to four seconds. Then, he breathes out for eight to 10 more. The inflow of air is about a third of the time as the outflow—that's what makes it effective—you're "purging" all of the stale out of your system by taking more time to breathe out. "Do that for a minute or two," he says, "and your blood is so oxygenated that you're prepared for anything.

Technique No. 2 is called "reset." Exhale all the stale air out and then take a big belly breath through your nose, slowly pulling it into your chest and filling your lungs to 100 percent capacity (for at least 10 seconds). Then, blow the air out through your mouth (for at least 10 seconds). Do this a minimum three times. Meanwhile, focus on breathing in all the energy out there—from the water or the trees. Tap into nature and receive all the energy that surrounds you. Then you're reset. Anything that you need at that moment will come to you. You're open to receiving it.

Garrett says the most important thing is to stay focused on the present and remember that you want what is best for everybody, and that this is your day.

Of course, he needed his years of preparation to get here. "If you know you're ready and you know you've done everything to prepare, you can stay in the moment and do what you do. Then, you can actually manifest things, make them happen; you see them happening, and they happen."

THINK MIRRORS, BELLY BREATHS AND SMILES

Mission

1. Look in the mirror. Position your legs as wide as your shoulders and stand up completely straight, but relaxed with no tension.

2. Stare into your own eyes until everything else melts away.

3. Begin the purge. Belly breathe in through your nose for two to four seconds and out through your mouth for eight to 10 seconds and continue staring into your own eyes.

4. Repeat.

5. Repeat and smile. Notice the difference in your mental state as you do this. Repeat a few more times.

6. Begin the reset. Feel your surroundings, where you are in the room and the sense of space. Create a moment of gratitude and love for this moment. It's the only thing that exists; it's the only thing that is real to you. Look deeper into your eyes, while taking in everything around you. Take a big belly breath through your nose, and then slowly pull it into your chest until your lungs are at full capacity (for at least 10 seconds). Every second and every bit of air make you stronger, more present, bigger, filling you with deeper gratitude for this moment as your smile lifts the muscles in your face, deepening your joy and presence. Blow the air out through your mouth (for at least 10 seconds) continuing to stare into your eyes. Blow it toward your image, empowering you further with a completely calm, but rock solid, sense of self.

Chapter 24: Join the Movement

You can change your mood physically to gain confidence, as well. It helps quell anxiety, while making you look stronger in a matter of minutes—or even seconds.

I've been in many dressing rooms with the band and dancers, when we've all dropped for pushups before a show. This works for reasons that change as the tour goes on. At first, the pushups disperse and exhaust nervous energy. They also pump up the muscles and veins—a bit of an ego boost.

As the tour progresses and the routine and confidence associated with the performance increases, the pushups serve as a stimulant—especially if we're engaged in a group pre-show nap. I remember being on the profoundly long Cher tour. Every night, I'd take a nice nap, get up sometimes as closely as 20 minutes before the show, splash water on my face, drop and pump out 50 to 80 pushups, stretch, pop on my stage clothes and be good to rock.

When I started playing with Scottish band Simple Minds in 1994, I ran regularly. The band invited me to record a batch of songs in their studio on Loch Earn. I'd run every morning before the session. This inspired band members Jim Kerr and Charlie Burchill to start running—and they got really addicted to it.

When we hit the road, they loaded a treadmill on one of the trucks to use every day. Jim, the lead singer, said it directly affected his performance. He'd run for 45 minutes before each show. Dripping with sweat, he'd rip off his workout clothes and throw on his stage clothes—no shower. It made him relaxed, intense and confident, like a top-class athlete.

Tony Robbins has a "power move"—no matter how anxious, nervous or tired he is, this sharp, physical movement brings him strength, resourcefulness and energy.

You probably already have one of these moves, but don't know it. Find a movement or movements that are unique to you that you associate with joy, happiness, power and confidence. This power move will create a shift in your physiology. Now, repeatedly practice it when you're in a positive mental state. Over time, your movement will become associated with happiness and focus. You'll be able to trigger these emotions on command.

My favorite power move now is to punch one arm straight out while hitting my chest open handed with the other and yelling, "PAH!" Then I repeat using the other arm as lead. It shocks my system, and it invigorates me. Disclaimer: Make sure whatever you create doesn't cause any discomfort.

Mission

Recall a time in your life when you felt great and exhilarated. How were you moving at that moment? Create a brisk and bold movement accompanied by a sound that represents that energetic and powerful feeling. Think about that great moment of exhilaration and make your power move. Do it at least 10 more times. Practice the move daily until you automatically associate the move with a great, powerful feeling.

I would be remiss if I didn't mention the benefits of exercise, especially in creating a confident performance.

People who regularly exercise feel less anxious and have less stress. Less stress means less distortion in your thought process—and less distortion leads to greater clarity. The same chemical reactions I mentioned earlier that occur with smiling also occur when you exercise. You feel better, more energetic and more in control of your body, and in turn your mind and emotions. Body image and the way you look at yourself directly affect your confidence. You can literally exercise the anxiety, frustration—even anger—from your system.

Additionally, the competitive urge to win allows you to take your frustrations out on an opponent (all with good intentions and in good spirit, of course). The competitive feeling (as confirmed by rapper Fong Sai U of The Roots) is a great way to foster confidence and bust through your nerves. It can give you edge, *chutzpah* and decisiveness.

Consistent exercise helps us stay in shape, look better and take pride in our bodies, which can inspire us to wear things that give us a deeper satisfaction in how we look. It makes us healthier and reduces or even eliminates the stress that is associated with feeling ill. It makes our immune systems less susceptible to things such as colds and flu and reduces the risk of heart disease, stroke, some cancers and other health problems.

Get into an exercise routine. It's a commitment to yourself, your craft, your team and your family. Everyone whose life you touch benefits from you honoring your body with exercise, sleep, a nutritious diet and careful consumption of anything that may impede your ability to perform.

Chapter 25: Know that the Joke's On You

One of Zappos CEO Tony Hsieh's first speeches was at a sales conference for UPS in 2004. He wrote his script beforehand, but he was also super nervous—so he faced it head on.

"I needed to push myself beyond my comfort zone. We were celebrating Halloween, and I specifically remember deciding to rehearse in a pimp outfit. It was bright fluorescent green, and my hair was fluorescent orange. Public speaking is something I had to force myself into; it was the same thing with that outfit."

If you can look yourself in the eyes while wearing a crazy outfit and deliver your presentation without a hiccup, you've darn well surmounted most distractions. That only builds your confidence. Doing something silly, shocking or extreme, particularly in the early stages of busting through fear, can also make the process of rehearsal more fun.

That's what ZDogg says. He's the internist-turned-speaker who's become an Internet celebrity known for his music videos, parodies and comedy sketches about contemporary medical issues and his work in the field. The career change makes him happy. He also understands stage fright from the medical standpoint.

"Your adrenal gland sees it as a fight or flight response. You perceive that you're in danger, your heart rate goes up, you perspire and your gut starts to cramp up. I understand the physiology of it. I know it's a primal response. I almost feel like I'm ticking off years of my life because I can feel my blood pressure rising and I can feel my pulse. I can tell this is maladaptive.

"Think about performance anxiety as a tiger in the wild. But you don't have the choice to run. You're forced to face the danger straight on. I realized early on that I could compensate for that by trying to be funny. I'd try to make jokes, distract the tiger if you will, and try to connect. I rehearsed jokes that would have a common resonance between the audience and me. If they were pre-meds, I was a pre-med at one point, let's make a joke about what incredible jerks pre-meds are or whatever. That worked, and I find that now, I'm still terrified, but only for the first 30 seconds of a presentation."

He remembers giving his graduate speech in 1999 at the University of California, San Francisco in front of 1,000 peers. It was one of the most terrifying moments of his life, standing in front of his equals and their families, his professors—and behind him, J. Michael Bishop, the Nobel Prize-winning chancellor of the school. "I said something very medical, because I was trying to put myself at ease. I said, 'Gosh guys, I really should have taken the beta blockers!' Everybody laughed, and then it all went OK."

(As a side note, drummer Stewart Copeland of The Police used beta-blockers in his early days, when the hours before the show were torture. "I really enjoyed playing shows the minute I was on stage. Why is it that I have to go through an afternoon of anxiety and emotional discomfort? It turns out, there's medication for that. The beta-blockers broke the cycle of show equaling nerves. Now, I can go into a show without any feeling of trepidation." Stewart says he rarely even needs them now. Note: Beta blockers cause a fluctuating heart rate and can potentially lead to congestive heart failure in extreme cases.)

Back to ZDogg, who says your preparation should always include understanding your audience's needs. But what if you have your "shtick" prepared and—surprise—your audience is three times older than you anticipated? ZDogg was booked for the San Francisco Surgical Society, and he misjudged the crowd.

"I show up, and there are 50 surgeons, with average age, probably 75. There were some 90 year olds adjusting their hearing aids. And here I am with a shtick that's designed for cynical young doctors, I start giving it, and I can tell these guys are not with me. Half of them can't hear me because their hearing aids aren't turned up."

He hit a wall when one of his mainstays fell flat. ZDogg had anticipated that moment after he arrived and saw the audience. He recalled that earlier, in the bathroom, he'd seen a Foley catheter, a device that few but old men would recognize. He had it stashed and held it up, made some silly remark and the old doctors chuckled. "I caught a stride and things started to pick up."

Sometimes humor can be an anchor to mend a previous anxiety—being able to laugh changes your association with an event permanently, as is the case when you do the Re-minding exercise in Chapter 7.

In Anatomy of an Illness, political writer Norman Cousins wrote about the power of laughter, humor and positive emotions as part of the treatment for his heart disease and reactive arthritis. He found that 10 minutes of jovial belly laughter gave him two hours of pain-free sleep.

Much later, in 2009, Dr. Lee Berk and his team of psycho-neuro-immunology (PNI) researchers at Loma Linda University Medical Center discovered that 30 minutes of funny videos a day gave heart patients fewer arrhythmias, lower blood pressure and lower stress hormone levels. They required lower doses of medication, and their ratio of repeat heart attacks was less than half that of a group that didn't watch funny videos.[8]

Similarly, Herbert Lefcourt, a psychologist from the University of Waterloo in Canada, studied humor and how its use could change emotional response to stress. Subjects reviewed recent stressful life changes as researchers monitored their negative mood disturbances. Lefcourt then infused humor, perception of humor and appreciation of laughter into their lifestyles. His results showed that the ability to sense and appreciate humor buffered the mood disturbances caused by negative life events.[9]

ACTION STEP:
EXAGGERATE UNTIL YOU BREAK

Mission
Think about your upcoming presentation. Find something funny about it, anything. Exaggerate it to the point of it looking, sounding, smelling or feeling quite ridiculous and larger than life. Start to laugh, and continue to laugh even though it may feel totally fake or contrived. Exaggerate it and keep laughing for at least two minutes, until it tires you out. How does that feel? Remember that vision to make you laugh whenever you want to release some negative emotion.

---

[8] http://www.sciencedaily.com/releases/2009/04/090417084115.htm

[9] H. Lefcourt, "Humor and Immune System Functioning," *International Journal of Humor Research* 3(3) (November 1990): 305-321.

Chapter 26: Relive a Success Experience

Ray Parker Jr. remembers hanging up on Stevie Wonder.

"*Music of My Mind* was my favorite album at that time, I'd never heard anything like that. I'd never even heard those sounds before, with a synthesizer. Before I could get nervous, I just didn't believe it was him, I actually hung up on him three or four times. He finally said, 'You know, we keep getting disconnected.' He was very kind."

Stevie asked Ray to come on tour with him, opening for The Rolling Stones, and they ended up collaborating on the song "Maybe Your Baby" for the album *Talking Book*. "Stevie said, 'You don't have to audition. I already talked to everybody, and they say you're my guy.'"

In the studio, Stevie heard the songs Ray was writing at the time, and he ended up producing some of them. The two even sang some duets together. That's when Ray really came into his own. That magical experience with Stevie Wonder built his confidence and reminded him of his success, and he could continually tap into that to stave off anxiety.

"When I left Stevie's band, people would say, 'You can't do this. You're not gonna be able to write hits.' I'm not even hearing that. Stevie Wonder spent three days of his own money and his own time working on my songs. I know I can write songs. I know I can. Even though everybody else in the industry said it's not possible, you know? I must be doing something right."

Losing sight of who we are and what we have done is an amnesia that can foster unfounded performance anxiety. Tap into your previous successes. It's not false confidence; it's a reality check because you've done it. These are the proven moments in which your clarity and capability have already worked. They're real confidence builders and can break down doubt and anxiety. When you're in this moment, the reasons for the anxiety are not important; a sense of resolve, relax and refocus are.

ACTION STEP:
REMEMBER THE TIME

Mission
Recall a time when you were clear, capable and confident about your performance. What made that experience great? What can you do to replicate it right now?

Matt Glowacki was born without legs; that never stopped him. He's a Paralympian, entrepreneur and public speaker—but his scariest moment came during something many of us can relate to—reinventing his career. He compares it to debuting a new album with a different sound—and no real way of knowing how fans will take the change.

For years, Matt was known as the "diversity guy" on the speaker's circuit…until his wife, Shannon, suggested a speech on happiness. It really resonated with him, because to talk about happiness, he would have to be authentically happy.

"The first thing I do is a little bit of visualization. Instead of worrying about what it's going to be like, I think about the last time I was successful and how that felt. That makes me have confidence in the material and in myself—that I can do the job. I have to find that place in myself."

Matt also calls his wife to tell her how he feels about her, and how she makes him feel, because so many of the characteristics of happiness come from how you interact with people in your life. "We share stories about our relationship, and the stories make me happy."

Finally, he tunes out everything negative and turns on the things that make him happy—he turns off the news and turns on the music. Matt loves the new happiness program. When he was the diversity guy that was how people related to him, based on common experiences. Now he's the happiness guy.

"I'm Mr. Smiles. They want to show me that they know what happiness is, too, so they bring the happiness themselves. It's easy to feed off that, and it just gets bigger and bigger. I basically tell them along the way that they're gonna be happy, and this is what happiness feels like. I grab them by the hand and help them along in the process."

Matt recalls a success experience every time he wakes up to motivate himself to get moving. "My life is about momentum. When I'm sitting there in the morning, and I turn on the TV, I make a decision that my momentum is going to stay in bed. But if I get up and do the things that I need to do in the morning, then I feel a bit of momentum to carry the day. I'm going down the hill, like a big wheel rolling. In the beginning, you have to push it to create energy, to create momentum. Thinking about what I need to do to prepare myself starts that momentum. Then, I get into the visualization, and the energy starts pulling me into the moment. When I start feeling the energy, that's where the magic is."

For musicians, this concept is like being in the groove when we play with a band. It makes me feel like I'm part of this flow and part of this energy, and I love it. I've heard athletes talk about the same thing, and I've witnessed partners pitching an idea to a potential customer and riffing off of each other. My manager, attorney and business partner, Stephen Stern, calls it "brain jamming" when we exchange ideas, feed off of each other and create a groove from that momentum that fosters confidence.

Chapter 27: Let Freedom Ring

When I reflected back on the Bad English audition a few years later, I realized something: I had amped up my chances of failure by focusing on not failing. This is a double-negative goal. It's like telling someone not to focus on a blue elephant. It's human nature to create an image in our minds and even manifest a goal because someone is drawing our attention to it or we are perpetuating a thought. By focusing on not failing, I inadvertently got exactly what I'd devoted so much energy to—failure. I had attached so much to the opposite outcome that it consumed me.

Exercise your freedom. I started working on being free to fail. This is not increasing your chances of failing; it is actually creating the opposite affect. When you realize you're free to fail, your anxiety about failing goes down. When you reduce your anxiety, you have less distortion in your thought process and you think with more clarity. All the physical manifestations of anxiety get reduced, as well. As you think more clearly, your body becomes more relaxed and you are more physically and mentally acute. This increases your potential to create your intended outcome—success. With that comes confidence.

I was freaking out about potential mistakes during drum master classes in front of audiences of 20 to 50 drummers, more so than when I played for 20,000 P!NK fans. So, I started changing my mindset, Re-minding. I exaggerated what would happen if I screwed up. I pictured falling off the drum still and breaking my arm and the crowd laughing wickedly as I got sucked into the ground by some gelatinous subterranean creature. The ridiculousness of the scenario made me laugh. At that moment, I got release and freedom from the stress that was binding me, leaving me free to focus on a fulfilling and magical performance.

Astronaut Alan Bean finds freedom by acknowledging that failure is intrinsic to being human. "Some days when you play, you're great. Some days you're average, and some days you're not as good as you wish you were, because that is the human condition, and you can't ever rise above the human condition. Pro athletes are just human. They drop balls; they get sick; they block the wrong person. You don't know it, but they know it, and their teammates know it.

"I burned out a TV camera when I was on the moon. Made a mistake. Pointed it at the sun. Boy, that was a terrible feeling. Took me a while to get over it and say, 'I'm just a human being. I did a lot of other things right. I didn't do that right, but I've got to stop worrying.' It's just something that humans have got to live with."

Baz Halpin's only in his early 30s, and he knows the importance of freedom. He has directed live and televised shows for Lady Antebellum, No Doubt, P!NK, Katy Perry, Sade, Swedish House Mafia, Tuna Turner, Usher—the list goes on. He sometimes has three projects going at once, which is a recipe for high anxiety.

"I've always just taken whatever opportunity came my way, rather than seeking out the opportunity," he says. "I never set out to be a director. When somebody said, 'Hey, do you want to try this or handle that,' I said, 'Sure.' I was never really afraid of failing, because it was never my goal to do it in the first place."

I've watched Baz work many times, and I've never seen him lose it. He's always ready to crack a joke and make people around him feel calm. It's ultra freedom. "I have the sense that I'm leading someone else's life, so I've never really taken it too seriously. When I'm physically doing a job, then it's a different person that takes over, and that person cares very much about not failing. But I know it's just my alter ego. I just carry out the task on that day in that place—it's very *now*. Then, you can't attach the prospect of what might happen should you fail in your task because there is no future."

Baz always shifts back to that place of freedom. "It's just a part of my psyche that only focuses on what's in that day. The other part of me, the guy who deals with the past and the future, he doesn't really care because he's not supposed to be doing my job in the first place."

In the days leading up to a show, Baz doesn't even think about it. By that point, it's pure focus, adrenaline. "Any anxiety or nervousness I have, I use to make my mind sharper. I react more quickly. It can make everyone so acute in a stressful situation."

Baz disassociates his emotions from the event to keep out fear and anxiety. The flip side of that is that he doesn't get the rush or the pleasure from the first show. Baz's satisfaction and feeling of triumph are delayed. He celebrates his victory weeks after that—after all the refinements have been made and he can really sit back and enjoy what he has co-created.

"Subconsciously, there's the side of your mind that worries about everything and feels the emotion. And because you separate out all that emotion to remove the fear and anxiety, you can't derive any positive emotion either—until you bring those two personalities back together. It's a defense mechanism."

Actually, he's only recently realized he does this. "If those two sides of my psyche bound together, I wouldn't be able to do what I do. The stress and the nerves of a million things that could go wrong—that fear would prevent me from doing anything. So, I separate myself from it emotionally."

When I asked NFL sideline reporter Laura Okmin how she finds freedom, she told me that she spends a minute corralling all her negative thoughts before she goes on air. "It's the opportunity to look really stupid in front of millions of people. I say one thing, and all of a sudden, everyone's going to go, 'Oh, she doesn't know what she's talking about.'

"I tap into the negative butterflies for a minute and think about everything that could go wrong, and I try to feel how awful that feels, 'You could look so stupid. You're not going to know what you're talking about.'"

And then, she turns it around, and taps into what she calls "positive butterflies." "You know what you're talking about. You're going to own this."

Former Fresno State field goal kicker Kevin Goessling has a miniature toilet, a gift from his sports psychologist. He uses it to remind himself to learn from the positives and "flush" everything else.

Actor Jeremy Piven finds his freedom through introspection. "What's nervousness?" he laughed. "It's energy. Your body is respecting what you're about to go through."

So, you panic and become subservient to that fear (which will negatively affect your performance) or you take a breath and work through it. Jeremy says, "It's a kind of 'OK-I'm-feeling-energy-that's-cool-it's-gonna-be-wild-oh-that's-alright-I'm-ready-let-me-breathe-through-this-moment' moment.

"You're probably already experiencing shortness of breath; you're nervous. So taking a breather actually serves a dual purpose. You'll even see the greatest fighters in the world—you'll even see Manny Pacquiáo—take deep breaths between rounds to slow their heart rates."

Celebrity chef Guy Fieri is free not to win, because he finds the silver lining in the situation. He relied on freedom when he was cast in *The Next Food Network Star*, his introduction to reality TV. It wasn't easy being the only contestant without a culinary school education. So, he asked himself, "What do I want out of this? If I don't win what are my wins? What are my potentials?"

Forget the fear. Guy examines the task at hand, sticks to the fundamentals that got him to that point and asks what he is trying to achieve. Five or so minutes before he goes on, he finds his own personal space, and reflects on the performance ahead. "I have to stretch, release my body and warm up, but that's just from watching the rock 'n' roll stars, that's from watching Sammy Hagar get ready to go."

Above all, he stays away from "success or death measures," instead choosing to focus on the journey and its incremental steps.

"I look at each situation in its entirety and use it as a stepping stone to get to the finale. That gives me a more consistent return and is a less-daunting task. It's like that old saying. 'What's the easiest way to eat an elephant? One bite at a time.'" (Remember Dr. Sol and firefighter Billy Hayes also talked about compartmentalizing).

You know the old cliché: It's not about the destination but about the journey. This has practical application in creating freedom and confidence. Over time, I've developed the ability to assume different viewpoints at different times and in different situations based on context and appropriateness. I've spent a great deal of time in this book concentrating on the importance of being acutely focused on your goal. I also suggest that it is vital to stop and observe—take a breath from the intensity. Reflect on the process and enjoy it.

Freedom, as defined by Merriam-Webster, is the absence of necessity, coercion or constraint in choice or action. Anxiety, on the other hand, is constraining, and limits your ability to foster clear choices. Stop every once in a while and observe. Enjoy this moment spent educating yourself in new techniques and greater confidence.

ACTION STEP:
GET IN THE MOMENT

Mission
1. *Think about being free to drop the goal of conquering your performance anxiety. Notice this moment right now—the sounds, smells, lighting, temperature, your body, your position, your mood, whether you are hungry or tired.*
2. *Hold it, own it, relax and observe.*
3. *Now, get free to dive in, conquer that anxiety and turn it into confidence! How does that feel?*
4. *Now, get free to fail at conquering the anxiety.*
5. *Now, be free to completely succeed and create complete confidence, until anxiety is a tiny twig you just crushed with your shoe.*

These "freedom flows" can be very powerful when you need a break from the goal, when you need time to reflect and be an observer of your own journey, to create a free mindset and celebrate the moment.

It is powerful and confidence building to be able to change your viewpoint at will. Having the freedom to change or shift your stand affects what you see and how you see it. Getting free to observe, fail and succeed are all examples of how you can shift your viewpoint. Freedom gives you the power of choice, of exercising your will and of being able to shift when you feel it's appropriate. Go ahead; celebrate your journey.

Chicago Bears kicker Robbie Gould does this every game. He knows that just one mistake, one miss, could cost him his job, even his career. A quarterback can throw a bad pass, a receiver can drop an easy ball, a defensive end can miss his tackle, but a kicker cannot miss a field goal. In that stress environment, it's hard for me to imagine how Robbie maintains his cool and his freedom—but he does.

"At the end of the day, if I don't perform, then guess what? My career's completely over. I'm in a sport where your average career is three years. So, if I'm only gonna play for three years, 16 games a year, I better enjoy those three years, because I don't know when my last game is gonna be my actual last game. I started taking the mindset of 'enjoy the ride and just have as much fun as possible, because you never know when it's gonna be over.' When you're thinking that you only have a certain amount of time to enjoy it, there's not enough time in the day to sit there and stress about what you can't do as opposed to what you're confident in doing and what you know you're able to do."

It calms me to know that even my friend, leadership coach Ronda Beaman, gets ridiculously nervous at a gig she's so frickin' good at it. "Every single time, whether there are two people in the room or 2,000 people in the room, I'm really sorry that I said I'd do it. I am always sick to my stomach, nervous, wishing I had gone into retail—anything besides having to go out and put myself up in front of other people for their judgment, enjoyment or whatever. I'm always sorry. I can listen to my introduction and the whole time in my head I'm going, 'What were you thinking?'"

Ronda takes comfort and finds her freedom in the stories of other great performers. She recalls watching an interview with Meryl Streep, who described the fear of just not being good enough. "On the airplane on the way to a new role, she's thinking all the way, 'I can't do it, I can't possibly do it! What did I think? I thought I had the talent to do this. What kind of stupid idea was that?' And she beats herself up all the way there. Then, she does her job, gets back on the plane, flies home and goes, 'Of course, I could do it. It was fabulous. It was easy!'"

Ronda is not about eradicating fear, but being free to have it, and harnessing it to create heightened awareness. She says people need to acknowledge that nervousness and that fear, know that it's going to be there and use it as the adrenaline and the juice for being good. "I don't think stage fright can be overcome by anyone. It has to be honored and worked through."

Fear is an important motivator, and it's also inspiring. It makes you feel alive, and it makes your awareness acute. If I have no fear when I go on stage, I feel like I'm dead. I want some—I just don't want it to overwhelm me to the point where I can't think or be effective. You just have to find the balance.

Ronda reminds her students that there's not a lot of difference in reaction between excitement and fear. Your palms get sweaty. You quiver. You feel a little sick to your stomach. Change your mindset. Believe in the excitement, not the fear. Your brain doesn't know the difference.

"It can change your whole first five minutes—and that first five minutes with an audience is crucial. You're honoring, not overcoming stage fright, and you're managing the emotion in a way that allows you to be your best. Use that as your knife's edge to be really, really on and gain confidence. Whether you're really excited or you're really afraid, your senses are heightened."

The metaphor I use is a roller coaster. I'm always scared when I'm going up the ramp. But the moment we start to go down, I get over that initial fear, and I always love it. I think of my stage performances like a roller coaster. I'm going up the roller coaster. 'Ladies and gentlemen, Mark Schulman!' Whoosh! Game on, no turning back.

Ronda boils it down further. "You have a choice every morning to get out of bed and yell, 'I'm back,' or to get out of that bed and go, 'Oh, another day.' It's all related to how you attack and appreciate every moment you're given. The bottom line: Feel the fear, and do it anyway."

It's really a simple choice.

Sax player Dave Koz offers a different take on Ronda's concept of using fear and nervousness. He actually likes getting nervous.

"It doesn't put me off, and it doesn't scare me away. And the nerves are only up until the point when I start to perform. I take it as a good sign that I'm alive. I'm doing something that is making me stand up and recognize that I'm alive and doing something in the world. It gives me that little spark."

Dave is gay. But as a kid, he didn't want to be. "It was like being a stranger in my own family, and I wasn't comfortable with those feelings, and basically I just shoved everything down." He wasn't free to be himself. That's a big challenge.

"I think that an inherent problem in our society is that people don't want us to be different. There's something terribly wrong with that, because we're all different, and we all have these wonderfully unique attributes that should be shared and celebrated. We shouldn't feel that paralyzing fear in those moments when we step up and say, 'Here's who I am,' with confidence. It's so foreign to us, and so scary to us, to actually publicly open ourselves up and be humble and show up as the beautiful gift that we are."

I love this about Dave, his passion and his willingness to see the beauty and uniqueness in others. He says that showing who you truly are should never be a negative experience. It can only be positive because you are being authentic. Authenticity inspires confidence. It may not look like you think it will, and you have to be flexible with what your response to that authenticity looks like.

"Every time you make yourself known in the world authentically, you'll be rewarded. You can always make things work for you. Like when people make mistakes or they start cracking up on *Saturday Night Live*, the audience just loves that. It's real. As long as you're free to be real they'll go with you anywhere."

That reminds me of some of the interactive performance seminars I've given for incarcerated kids in the Los Angeles area. I'm really just there with good intention, and I tell them that right away. And I always sense a shift in some of them, because they get it. Most of these kids have been abused or neglected, so when someone shows real interest, concern and kindness, they respond.

Recently, during one of my drumming events, my gear kept breaking down. I had to laugh it off and be free. Before that, it was the white elephant in the room. So, I just brought up. "Everything's breaking, but we're all friends. Right?" I broke the tension, and the audience started engaging and laughing. I was not only free to have the gear break, but free to talk about it.

My friend, Vivian Campbell of Def Leppard, was playing a guitar solo with Whitesnake at Wembley Arena in 1988. He was alone on stage, and he wasn't using a wireless. He was standing in front of the drum riser, and didn't realize that his foot was on the cable.

"I'm not exactly sure how it happened. My cue was to start there, and then go downstage center. I was on an angle, the momentum carried me forward and, because I was somehow wrapped around the guitar cable and it was through the guitar strap, it pulled the guitar strap off and the guitar went flying into the pit.

"That was the hardest thing I've ever had to recover from onstage. I'm out there alone; it's not like the rest of the band can deflect. So, I had to go to the side of the stage, get another guitar and come back onstage and continue the solo."

He says onstage challenges can actually spur you into a higher gear. You have no recourse in those situations. "You can either crawl under a rock, or you can pump it up. It's your choice."

Remember that knowing you have a choice in any situation is what creates your viewpoint of freedom and washes the anxiety away.

My former band mate Kelly Hansen of Foreigner says you have to ask yourself why you're afraid. If you're worried about making a speech in front of a crowd, ask yourself what will happen if you fail. Is there a name you are afraid to mispronounce or a sentence that ties your tongue? What's the worst thing that can happen? In most cases, you'll find the consequences are pretty marginal. Kelly understands that the more you're free to fail, the better your chances of success.

"Once you realize that, you can minimize the impact of fear, because you know that no matter what happens, it's not really going to be that bad. If you're a sweaty person, bring out a napkin and dab yourself along the way. You can always find solutions to problems. Most people in the audience know that you're doing something that for most people is unusual and difficult. As Franklin Roosevelt said: 'The only thing we have to fear is fear itself.'"

Zappos CEO Tony Hsieh is actually most nervous when he talks to his own employees, because there's so much at stake, and it's not rehearsed. It's not a speech he's done hundreds of times. Phil Carson learned a trick to combat that exact thing. Phil is one of the most accomplished record executives in history. His signings include AC/DC, ABBA and Yes. Phil had to answer to one of the godfathers of the music business, Ahmet Ertegun, the founder of Atlantic Records, and recalls a specific sales force presentation from that time.

"I was really nervous. I had worked really hard on it, and I'd actually been through some fairly serious corporate training. I'd learned that if you're going to make a speech, you put the cards in the order that you want train-of-thought to be established, and you put little headlines, so that you know what you're doing. And I worked particularly hard on this speech with my then-wife—days we were at it. I happened to be at a meeting with Ahmet. He sees me shuffling through these cards, and he says, 'What are you doing?'

"I said, 'Well I've got a series of points I want to make, and I want it to be right.'

"He says, 'These people work for you. You don't have to worry about what they think. They're your employees. Why should you care?'

"And I took those as words of wisdom, and even though I still went out with those cards that day, I had absolutely no nerves whatsoever."

Of course, you *should* care about your employees. I think Ahmet really just wanted to shock Phil out of his anxiety. It made him less attached to the outcome that in turn created freedom for him. And it worked.

"Ahmet's theory of public speaking was to know what you're going to talk about, have someone else write a speech and then throw it away. He'd just get out there, and he'd make it up as he went along anyway. The freedom gives you the confidence that you're not going to mess it up."

Phil says when you're free to trust your instincts and put yourself out there, then you'll be more relaxed, and fantastic things can come to you. He remembers talking about a new band called AC/DC in the early 1980s. At the time, he says, the big hit was Frankie Goes to Hollywood. A German girl named Nina Hagen had a record called "99 Red Balloons." "I said, 'When Nina Hagen's 99 red balloons have all burst and Frankie has been sent back to Hollywood, AC/DC will still be rocking.' And that carried around the world, because it was the right thing to say."

Phil says if you're confident about your vision, your anxiety will disappear. "If you believe in yourself and the decision that you've made, and you have the ability to stick with it, you do so. I signed AC/DC to a 15-album deal for $25,000. The 15th album got sold to Atlantic for $10 million, so it was pretty good. But in the beginning nobody gave a damn. They thought I was crazy."

I've been performing at seminars and giving speeches for 20 years, and each time, I spend a week practicing my set over and over to perfect phrases and transitions.

One time, preparing for a speech to some college students, I became obsessed with the details of my articulation and wording. The preparation was actually making me anxious and obsessive. My mentor, Jim, reminded me that I'd given many successful speeches before and suggested that for a change (and fun) I stop practicing and rely on spontaneity, experience, personality and my relationship with that particular audience.

He was right. I needed to be free to allow my hours of rehearsal to run the show. And it worked...for a few days...until I began to regress into old habits, compulsively going over words, phrases and concepts. By Day 3, I saw the negative progression, and, to stop it, I tried to force myself to have fun with the process. And I lightened up a bit, even if I didn't truly embrace the freedom.

But on stage the day of the speech, I was stiff. I sensed it was going pretty well, but I just wasn't in the groove. I couldn't embrace my freedom to be impulsive. At one point, I obsessed about one passage so hard my mind went blank. I walked back to the podium to get a drink of water, forced a laugh and asked the audience for questions. I stood there, feigning confidence and staring at the students like I'd planned it, inside hoping for something to say.

Then something cool happened, a wave of calm and inspiration. I recalled the discussion we had about me being free to let things happen organically and I just let go. I started involving the audience in spontaneous ways. They lit up. The more impromptu I became, the more the audience responded. I opened up, and started storytelling, letting the learning points just...surface. I engaged with audience members, instead of talking at them.

Magic ensued! Super-groovy improvisation. I was free to let my preparation, my capability and my audience create a confident and successful presentation. I know it worked because I got asked back the next year to do the same event.

Freedom gives you the power to allow some magical outcomes that you might not have even envisioned. Tony Hsieh recalls an example of this. "I tell people about one of my favorite TV shows growing up, *MacGyver*. The reason why I loved that show is because he would somehow figure out how to take a rubber band or some duct tape and string and turn it into a sailboat. You may not know exactly how, but by the end of the hour, he would figure it out."

And that's what he loves about being an entrepreneur. He gets to play MacGyver every day. He's free to take chances, experiment and trust others.

Tony also surrounds himself with the right people—such as Fred Mossler, who joined Zappos in 1999, and was recently promoted to the position of "no title" from senior vice president of merchandising, mainly because they couldn't think of a designation for him. Mossler shares an interesting story about confidence.

At one point during his conquest of Mexico, Spanish explorer Hernán Cortés scuttled his ships to disallow retreat. "The armies stood on the shore watching the ships burn and said, 'What are you doing? How are we going to get back to Spain?' He said, 'Well, we shouldn't worry about that. Now, all we have to worry about is how to move forward.'"

Confidence goes a long way even if those around you are more aligned with fear.

Remember Kelly G., the cancer conqueror, and her hospitalization in Portugal? She had a fever of 103.5 Fahrenheit and was alone (the staff sent her producer Anita Tibau back to the hotel). Late that first night, seven people barged into her room.

"They tell me they're going to put a main-line catheter in my neck." She has seriously damaged veins due to prior chemotherapy, and that could be extremely dangerous. "They're going to do all this stuff to me, and I can't communicate to them that I'm scared to death that they're going to rip a hole in the vein in my neck. I don't know how to communicate about how many times I've had a cancer, how many IVs I've had and how many catheters I've already had in my neck; it's not translating.

"I realized that this might be the last time I talk to anybody, because I don't have a phone. Nobody knows I'm in the hospital. It's a scene in a movie. At that moment, I just had to get OK with the freedom that I might not be here anymore, and I'm free to go. That's some serious freedom to generate. I'm free to die."

ACTION STEP:
BE FREE TO … BE

Questions
1. *What performance are you free NOT to give?*
2. *What performance are you free to give?*
3. *What success are you free NOT to have?*
4. *What success are you free to have?*
5. *As a performer…*
   - *What are you free to be?*
   - *What are you free to do?*
   - *What are you free to have?*

Chapter 28: Get To

We have a way of forgetting how wonderful life can be. We think about all the things we have to do, and our minds create a trap—it all becomes drudgery. Try shifting your thinking from what you have to do to what you get to do. Change the way your brain operates. You'll feel a lot differently about the experience; it simply becomes more fun.

You may think that you have to do these things, but the reality is that you do not have to—there's always something else you can do instead. If you consciously chose to do it, then you can create a new sense of value in your life, of free will. This is your life you have worked to create. Take pride in it. Value the little things that you have taken for granted as things that are simple pleasures—to experience, not to be taken for granted. Quit taking yourself so seriously and getting trapped by your have-to mentality.

As humans, we prize freedom. We want to feel we have a choice in what we do. If you take responsibility for your life, everything you do becomes a choice. You may think that you have to go to school, but if you get to go to school, you get to have an education, you get to have a better job and you get to have a better life. You see the consequences, and this entices your sense of freedom. If you realize that your life can be about the decisions that you are free to make and the choices you are creative enough to cultivate, you change your attitude. This enhances your appreciation of how truly enjoyable your life can be.

ACTION STEP:
GET IN THE MOMENT

Mission
Think of three things you feel like you have to do (take your car to the shop, work out, mow the lawn, go to the market, work). Write them down. Now shift your attitude from "have to" to "get to."

This works well for processes that are vital to your success that you currently take for granted, such as doing a financial report, preparing an agenda for a meeting or rehearsing your keynote speech in the mirror. Shift your viewpoint and view these activities as a privilege instead of a chore. I could view practicing drumming rudiments as a painstaking process. Instead, I choose to see it as a privilege. Also, the many hours I spent refining these core skills has gifted me my extreme capability to not only express myself in an artistic way, but to make a handsome living doing something that I still love doing.

Pay attention to your words; next time you notice yourself saying that you have to do something, shift it to get to.

Chapter 29: Have a Little Faith

Faith is adjunct to—not a substitute for—real capability. It's not going to make you more confident; you are as good as you are, no better, no worse. If your confidence is based on your capability, then it's true confidence.

That said, if you build your trust/faith on evidence or proof—you have practiced, rehearsed and performed and therefore you trust your abilities—then you are back to simply being capable. Faith as it relates to a successful performance or presentation is the result of confidence that is a result of capability.

I've seen confidence used interchangeably with faith by definition, but it's the direct result of developing capability. That's why it can be dangerous to align this concept with the concept of faith alone because faith by itself can be blind. This gets us into the realm of false confidence, and that can be a dangerous place to hang out.

Having noted this, I interviewed some people who put a high stake in faith as a way to stave off stage fright.

Drummer Denny Seiwell is one of them. He's is best known for Wings, but he should be known for so many other things: his first real gig at the Half Note Jazz Club jamming with the Zoot Sims/Al Cohn Quintet, performing with The Who and the London Symphony Orchestra in rock opera *Tommy,* playing with the orchestra in some of James Newton Howard's most difficult movie scores. ("If you listen to *Waterworld*," he said, "you can hear my lips moving to the beat.")

Denny talks about his defining moment—a private audition in New York with Sir Paul McCartney for Wings. McCartney just told him to go ahead... play some rock 'n' roll.

"I played some shuffles. I played a half dozen grooves for him. We laughed, we talked and he said, 'That's good, man.' And I went home figuring I ain't never gonna get this gig. Three days later the phone rings. 'Hello, this is Paul. Would you like to make a record with me?'"

Denny said, "'Let me check my book...yeah, yeah, I can do it.'"

He's had a few scary moments, and he's even had significant challenges, despite the fact that he's one of the most accomplished drummers in the world. He recalls working on one of James Netwon Howard's pieces.

"They're really scary scores. And I'm playing a bass drum part, and it's really awkward. We take a break. The whole orchestra is awkward. It's really a hard piece of music. I go in the booth with James, and he says, 'You're not making it.' I said, 'What? I know it's hard, but I can make it.' He said, "Well, give it another two run-throughs, and then if you don't get it, I'm gonna say, 'We're gonna go with the other plan.' I'm not gonna embarrass you in front of the orchestra."

Two takes later, Bob Zimmitti came in to play the bass drum part—Denny played a different instrument. "He played it right, but he played it so loud, they had to do another take. And he turns around to me. 'You better not ever do that to me again.' And that was the only time I felt a little embarrassed that I couldn't actually do one of those. James said, 'Look, I wrote this thing, but I can't even play it.'"

But it wasn't the end of the world. And that's what's so great about Denny's attitude—he says that he has faith in himself to be the best he can be. No more, no less, and people like that.

"Now that I'm sober, I let a lot of crap go. I just have faith and give it to God and say, 'Thanks for allowing me to be here for this situation. And if my good isn't good enough, so be it. Maybe they won't call me next time, but I'm never alone. I remember the first time I sat down to play, sober. You know, I used to do a lot of crazy stuff. Before we played, we'd go in the alley and have a few tokes and some drinks. I sat down with my blues band down at Residuals with Sweet Grease, and I said a little prayer. It was probably one of the best nights in my life."

Celebrity chef, Guy Fieri from *Top Chef* and Food Network was managing restaurants in Southern California, and doing quite well at it, in the late 1980s. But by the mid-1990s, he was ready for a new challenge. So he left Los Angeles with a pregnant wife, $5,000 in his pocket, two dogs and a Hyundai with 200,000 miles on it (that he'd had since college) with plans to open a restaurant in wine country. To help fund the venture, his mom and dad mortgaged his childhood home.

There was a lot riding on his success; and in the restaurant business, you only get one shot. In 2006, Johnny Garlic's launched in Santa Rosa to great success, but Guy doesn't cite luck—he cites faith.

"You really gotta believe, because if you second-guess yourself, if there's any weak link, there's a strong possibility it will be exposed. I surrounded myself with my friends, my family and God and got focused, set a game plan and went and kicked its ass and haven't looked back since."

Chapter 30: Find Power in Routine

Canadian golfer Frank Corby decided to go pro several years into his career as a club professional. He still remembers the make-or-break event, a fall qualifier at the course where he's currently employed (the Royal Ashburn Golf Club in Toronto). It was September, and the players saw every type of weather: rain, sun, fog. And the outcome of his play wouldn't affect just him; it would affect his family and his financial supporters.

"That absolutely added extra pressure to do well, not just for myself, but to show them that their decision to financially support me made sense." And that moment lasted over the course of four days. "I had to be level-headed and walk that fine line, where you don't get too excited or too down because there will still be the next hole or next round to play."

Every hole, every drive was a difference-maker. Even after professionals join the tour, golf only pays on a what-have-you-done-lately scale. If you don't play well enough, you don't get paid—at all.

But Corby says he doesn't really get "stage fright." He gets a few butterflies, a bit of tension through his shoulders and his hands.

His reason: Confidence in his routine.

"In reality, it's just another day. I would get up X amount of hours before my tee time. I don't ever want to feel rushed. I don't perform well when I'm hurried or out of my routine. I have a good breakfast and just relax a little bit if I can, and arrive at the golf course to check in and warm up appropriately—just going through the routine—and 10 to 15 minutes prior to my tee time, I'll go to the first tee and be ready to go."

Champion poker player Vanessa Selbst, known for unconventional strategy and risky moves, relies on routine as well to settle her nerves, especially when the stakes are high—on Day 3 or 4 of a tournament when she can't eat or sleep or when her every move is televised and scrutinized by her peers. She remembers these situations acutely, like a disastrous game in late 2010.

"I hadn't played cash games in a really long time, so I was pretty rusty and extremely nervous going in. I usually try to take it easy and figure out the table early on, but for some reason I played one of the worst hands I've ever played on the third hand. I basically couldn't fold pocket queens when it should have been very obvious that this amateur had a better hand than me. And I lost $200,000 on that hand, and I actually only brought $400,000 with me, so I had already lost half of what I had come to play with."

She never fully recovered.

There's a phenomenon in poker called tilt, in which players let a poor decision affect later plays, their heads get so clouded that they basically can't make any optimal decisions. The levels of tilt vary from minor to full-blown. In poker, tilt is the worst sort of performance anxiety.

"If you hesitate, then all of a sudden you're second-guessing yourself—because now you're thinking, 'Well, I waited too long. Now, if I bet, they're gonna see right through me. They're gonna know it's a bluff.' And you talk yourself into not making the right plays. It's a spiral like that, and that's what happened to me."

It's difficult to ebb the tide mid-game. But it's the routine that helps Vanessa.

"It's just remembering that it's the same thing you've done every single time, like you've done every day getting there," she said. Recovery depends on the strength of the table, how much money is on the line and the extent of the nervousness. The groove returns usually at the advent of a mildly unconventional play, something that comes naturally to Vanessa, and something that reminds her of how good she actually is.

Firefighter Billy talks about the confidence mask test, the ultimate Fire Academy test. "You would wear your firefighting gear and the breathing apparatus with a complete blackout face piece. You would have to make your way through a maze. You're crawling under stuff. You're climbing over stuff. You're trying to wedge yourself within small environments.

"They're putting you in scenarios where you're getting wedged—you're actually getting trapped. They're also intentionally entangling you to see how you react and how you untangle yourself. You have to remove your mask and untangle yourself and put it back on before you can continue to go. If you can't pass the mask confidence course, you fail out of the academy."

We all need enough clarity and capability to pass our own mask confidence course.

Chapter 31: Just Show Up

In a 2008 interview with Collider.com, Woody Allen said: "I made the statement years ago, which is often quoted, that 80 percent of life is showing up. People used to always say to me that they wanted to write a play, they wanted to write a movie, they wanted to write a novel, and the couple of people that did it were 80 percent of the way to having something happen. All the other people struck out without ever getting that pack. They couldn't do it, that's why they don't accomplish a thing, they don't do the thing, so once you do it, if you actually write your film script, or write your novel, you are more than half way towards something good happening. So that I was say my biggest life lesson that has worked. All others have failed me."

A friend of mine who worked in the *American Idol* camp told me about a kid who had gone to auditions for three seasons, but only walked through the door on his fourth. The power of showing up and doing the work can fuel your confidence. Even with simple tasks—like going to the gym—if I can just get myself there, I already feel a sense of accomplishment. The workout is rarely as hard as I anticipated.

Performance anxiety is a form of situational anxiety, or the fear of taking action. View the ability to show up and work as a privilege. You have the opportunity to experience anxiety, because you're doing something that matters to you.

I'll let you in a secret fear of mine: missed opportunity. It's a ship in the night with a billion dollars of gold and diamonds that could have been yours, but you didn't see it in the dark. Look at the cost of avoiding something because of anxiety. If you knew it could have a billion dollars—wouldn't you try harder to see that ship?

We were in Cleveland for the fourth show of Cher's 2002 *The Farewell Tour*. We set up as usual behind a white scrim on stage, listening to the intro music while Cher climbed onto her chandelier (modeled after a fixture in her own home). The curtain fell, and we dove into "Still Haven't Found What I'm Looking For." The band was slammin.' The only thing missing was Cher.

One by one, everyone stopped playing and singing. All eyes were fixed above the stage, where all we could see were Cher's dangling feet. How was she suspended in mid-air? Was she alive? It was the most frightening moment of my 25-year touring career.

Of course, it didn't take long for the audience to catch on. We were quite the spectacle of frozen musicians. Then…mayhem. Men in the audience whimpering in their Cher costumes. Her manager and assistants, all the crew ran on stage. Her sister, Georgann, was hysterical.

Apparently, her waist harness had inadvertently attached to a metal truss behind her above the stage. When the platform came down, she didn't. She was left hanging 40 feet above the stage by that thin metal harness.

The head rigger couldn't get her down. So, the operator raised the chandelier until Cher was able to regain her footing and unhook herself. We all watched, breathlessly. At one point, the platform dropped, and she nearly lost her footing. A unified gasp echoed throughout the arena.

She made it down unscathed, and her entire entourage was there to greet her as she got off the platform. They walked her off the stage, and, as she passed by me, I could see fear in her eyes. We waited on stage for what seemed like a lifetime. The empty mic center stage was a lonely reminder of a near catastrophe that might usurp the tour.

I wondered what was going to happen. Was this the end of the show? The end of the tour? Did I need to find another gig? I unplugged my in-ear monitors and began preparations to leave the stage.

And then Cher came storming out and grabbed the mic. The audience roared. She yelled, "Let's do this again!" She was on fire, and I never saw her give a more energized and inspired performance. That choice to come back reflected a career of "the show must go on." That tour, slated for just three months ran nearly three years, grossed more than $300 million and put us on record as the longest tour in history for a female artist. Think of the joy, inspiration, entertainment and immeasurable amounts of sequins that would have been missed!

Cher used that experience as the foundation for her monologue every night. Home girl had a great time with it. She developed a whole routine. She described how she felt like a "drag queen piñata." She joked about hanging by a metal thread, about the overwhelming urge to pee—the only things stopping her, a $50,000 Bob Mackie gown and the next day's headlines.

Cher could have allowed the reality of the experience to overwhelm her. She did just the opposite. Any other fears she might have had were overshadowed by the actual spectrum of death. She embraced her bravery and used it to empower herself. And she just showed up.

SECTION 4: ONE LAST STORY

I'd like to end with the story of Kelly Gallagher, living proof of the power of clarity, capability and confidence. But she wasn't fighting anxiety; she was fighting for her life.

Chapter 32: Three Cs For Life

It's 1991, and I'm in love. I've found some permanent bliss in a relationship. I'm nearly 30, and after many long relationships—and witnessing the marriages of several friends—I'm also in love with the idea of a lifetime with someone.

Three months in and smitten, I give Kelly a passionate kiss and board a plane from Los Angeles to Portland, my old stomping grounds, for some R&R and a bit of rock 'n' roll. I'm hanging with my mates, basking in old times and singing the praises of new life, love and the completion of my first big rock tour (with Richard Marx).

Then, I get a call that set the precedent for many tears of my life. Kelly is crying. Her acupuncturist just found a pretty sizable lump on her abdomen.

It's not a new experience for her. Nearly 10 years ago her friend's sister, a nurse, noticed that one side of Kelly's neck looked larger than the other. She went for a checkup and was promptly diagnosed with Hodgkin's disease (lymphatic cancer) Stage 2 (the mildest stage). Her mom pulled her out of engineering school, and, at 20 years old, Kelly was subject to immediate and regular radiation treatments.

With this latest news, I'm shocked, stunned and get on the next flight home. Kelly has no health insurance. We go to the doctor and pay for an MRI out of pocket. The mass in her abdomen is a softball-sized tumor. Kelly is aghast; there had been no symptoms.

The doctor is big and bushy, white haired, loud, aggressive—and adamant that she gets an immediate bone marrow extraction to complete his diagnosis. He gives her a local anesthetic and proceeds to manually drill into her hip to extract marrow from the bone. She screams in pain with each twist of his wrist, squeezing my hands so tightly that the circulation starts cutting off.

I don't dare move. I'm nearly in tears. The 15-minute process feels like 15 hours. I can see that it has scared Kelly away from conventional doctors. There's good news, though, the cancer is not in her bone marrow. It's Hodgkin's Stage 3.

It feels like that drill extracted my "happily ever after" along with her marrow. But it never crosses my mind to bail on Kelly; her battle with cancer is now mine, too.

A chasm exists between that which is controllable, and that which is not. That chasm is where fear lives, where it brews and festers, sometimes causing your body to go into shock; it numbs and protects you, giving you a reprieve from reality. It's like dropping into Level 1 (unconscious incompetence), a safe haven from the fear.

I'm running one day, crying and accelerating to a nearly unbearable speed, believing at some level that the harder I run, the better the chances that my girlfriend will beat the beast. I'm chanting to myself over and over, "She's gonna live!" By the time I get back to our apartment, I'm desperately exhausted and barely able to breath or stand. I see Kelly and shout to her, "You're gonna live!" She looks at me, disappointed, and says, "Of course, I'm gonna live."

I'm embarrassed, but empowered, too. This whole time, I've been associating cancer with death. Fear is vast and complex, and so much of it is based on the unknown. The only way to dissipate it is through clarity and knowledge.

And I see a solution, the antidotes of fear: knowledge and clarity. Knowledge is the power to make the unknown known; the learning curve may be steep, but it's surmountable. Clarity comes as the result of knowledge, enabling you to take action based on what you learn. There's subjectivity in what combination of ideas, choices and actions result in healing.

I've only known cancer once before; my grandfather died of the disease, but I was too young to embrace the actuality of how he died. This time, cancer's on the front lines of my life. And with it come sleepless nights, desperate and highly affectionate attempts to console, meditation, dubious prayer, stress-reduction exercises and countless sessions with my mentor, Jim Samuels. And there's no better way to combat cancer and the financial challenges it brings than through tenacity, research clarity, action and a whole lot of love.

We opt to explore many options and viewpoints about her disease, opening the channels of belief, hope and self-empowerment to give her the capability to move her body to a point of balance. We investigate a variety of mostly alternative therapies, mainly due to their comparatively low cost. The knowledge is giving us clarity; the clarity is giving us options.

Kelly researches and tries raw food and wheat grass implants down in San Diego, a strict macrobiotic diet augmented with visits to a Chinese herbalist and acupuncturist and other ever more esoteric treatments—even an ozone body bag. We look into a Dr. Gonzalez and his enzyme therapy, and Kelly flies to New York two days later to meet him.

There's a difference between conventional medical treatment and this type of "alternative" therapy, which requires patients to be engaged in the process of their healing. Active involvement in the treatment empowers patients, enabling them to use their own capabilities to take action, and gives them a sense of control and in turn, confidence. It gives them a strong belief not only in the program but also in their decisions to implement it.

Kelly continues therapy with Dr. Gonzalez for a few years, as I tour and record with Bobby Caldwell, Foreigner and Simple Minds. Dr. G says she's getting better. Her regimen becomes an integral part of our lives. We're traveling the world, having fun and doing our best to stay hopeful, disciplined and healthy.

Kelly is constantly educating herself and assembles a team of friends and contacts across the globe to support her alternative-health treatments. She incorporates some pretty esoteric practices into her enzyme therapy. To me, some of it reeks of quackery, but I endorse anything she does, as long as things keep improving. But they don't.

Regardless of what Dr. G says, Kelly gets weaker. We have blood work done at Cedars-Sinai in West Hollywood and her red cell count is extremely low. Oncologist Leland Green strongly encourages us to start conventional chemotherapy treatment, but Kelly's resistant.

She undergoes a blood transfusion, and feels like a million bucks. I'm losing faith in Dr. G's program, but she continues, and her health declines, necessitating several more transfusions. I move us out of Hollywood to an apartment right on the water in Malibu, hoping that the environment will stimulate further healing. It's obvious that we need to do something.

At this point, even my mother is demanding that we go see Dr. Green. I know Kelly sees this as defeat, but we all know it's inevitable. We set up an appointment. Dr. Green's prognosis is not good: The cancer has escalated to Stage 4. The lymphoma has metastasized into her bones.

Kelly agrees to start a full course of chemotherapy, but insists that she continue her various adjunct therapies, including having some of her alternative healers visit Dr. Green's office. This allows her to participate in her healing, and it deepens her capability. She uses the adjunct therapies in coordination with the conventional one, and this gives her confidence in getting better.

I'm on the road off and on, and miss her first treatment. Her friends John and Sheri transport her to the hospital in West Hollywood and back to our Malibu apartment.

Kelly's a distinctive mix of charm, rebellion, tenacity, entitlement, gratitude and empathy. She was a competitive swimmer, and at times, seems to thrive on the challenge of the disease, taunting and charming her doctors and nurses at the same time. She willingly accepts the chemo IV, but only if the doctors and nurses endure her soliloquies on augmenting these "toxic" treatments with nutrition and adjunct therapies. She's both lovable and a royal pain in the ass. Through it all she exhibits an amazing display of clarity and confidence.

Kelly rarely complains about the physical cost of chemo, even in 1994 when that cost is high. She's sick, drowsy and unmotivated. The doctors prescribe Marinol (a pharmaceutical form of marijuana's primary active ingredient, THC), but it renders her paralyzingly high. She decides that smoking good old fashion reefer allows her more clarity and control, and she actually finds substantial relief from most of her symptoms. She gains a little weight, keeps food down and actually enjoys the taste.

In the thick of all this, I get hired to play the Billy Idol song "Speed" on the movie soundtrack. I spend the next eight years intermittently recording, playing live and co-writing some songs with Billy and his guitar player, Steve Stevens.

I buy Kelly a truck that she really wants—small consolation for her pain. Her hair is falling out in clumps—in the shower, in the bed, on her hairbrush. We're driving to one of my rehearsals when she starts crying inconsolably. I pull the car over but there is nothing I can say; I just hold her until she calms. Kelly assures me that she's OK. She apologizes; I tell her she's entitled to it. We share an intense hug; I get out of the truck and watch her drive away.

After rehearsal, I wait outside and watch as her truck drives up. I don't recognize the driver. My heart drops as it passes me and parks. I'm thinking that something must have happened to Kelly; they've sent someone to pick me up.

I rush forward and am shocked to see that it is Kelly. Her hair is short, spiky and bright blonde. She runs up to me with the energy of a child and jumps in my arms. We kiss and then start laughing until we cry.

She's so happy and oozing with pride. I ask what happened; she boldly replies, "I was sick and tired of being sick and tired. I had an epiphany when I was driving. Instead of thinking that I have to lose my hair, I decided to see it as I get to have a new hairstyle!"

First of all, she looks hot. Second of all, she's happy. This is the first time I really understand the power of shifting a "have to" to a "get to", and how it can alter your body and confidence. We get in the car, and she insists on driving. She is more energetic and released than I've seen her in months. We decide to rent a few movies, go home, make dinner and just celebrate life. We make a rockin' meal, leave all the dishes dirty and retire to the bedroom with the cache of movies. We fall asleep peacefully.

The next morning, I had made an agreement to workout with my buddy, Dan. I even think to myself, "Ugh, I have to work out with Dan." And I catch myself. I need an attitude shift. I get to work out with Dan. I suddenly feel invigorated and excited about the process. I look at the dishes and think, "Wow I have to clean all these dishes." I stop and smirk as I reflect on why I'm cleaning these dishes, thinking about our lovely night, the intentional reckless abandon of leaving the dishes. I never had such a great attitude about doing dishes.

Kelly makes it through Round 1 of chemo. Her body responds favorably, and her blood scores improve. She comes on the road with me to record an album with Simple Minds at the band's studio on Loch Earn in Scotland. We are triumphant, celebratory and cautious. She is still engaged in a strict regimen of adjunct rituals such as coffee enemas, a variety of pills and a specific diet (though there's some food partying going on occasionally). We rent a car in London and drive through England into the Scottish Highlands. Kelly drives, bold and cocky, and at a few points, scares the hell out of me.

•　　•　　•　　•　　•

I watched Kelly employ the Three Cs to win her war. Her clarity and focus about the people and methodologies she wanted to engage in her healing were impenetrable. Her commitment to preparation was inexhaustible. Her near-constant research, assimilation of supporters, calculated defiance of conventional medicine and doctors—even her addiction to stimulants to create energy when she organically had none—kept her one step ahead. Her human GPS was like the most powerful computer-navigated weapon, crunching numbers and obliterating problems with eccentric solutions the rest of us wouldn't even recognize—all because her goal of survival was solid.

She developed an astounding capability of employing seemingly crazy therapies alongside a rigid and profoundly difficult conventional protocol. This surrounded her in a shield of confidence. Kelly rehearsed her worst-case scenario through her freedom to die. This reduced her fear, and the stress associated with the disease. It calmed her, and that calm affected her chemistry and enabled her to heal more easily, which increased her chances of living. She was altruistic and audience-centric. During her most trying times in the hospital, she would fraternize and entertain patients, learning their wants and dreams; even when she was hanging on by a thread, she shared energy with them.

She brought half the office to every chemo session to focus away from the toxicity and on whatever project she was engaged in. And her visualizations about what she still needed to do in life allowed her to plow through adversities.

What I've Concluded

I wrote this book lying beside the Eiffel Tower in Paris on my iPad, lounging in a dark dressing room at a casino in Canada, during a break onstage for rehearsals with P!NK and while getting caffeinated in Starbucks cafés across the globe.

I interviewed people in restaurants and bars and in dressing, hotel, living and meeting rooms—even once on a yacht. I Skyped from my office and studio, various hotel rooms, coffee shops and patios. My life of travel and high audience exposure is a unique one, and it's given me a bold, worldly perspective. It's allowed me to gain the varying viewpoints of some wonderful people whose lives may have very little in common with mine, except our shared experiences of performance.

Every interview yielded special moments and cool circumstances. One of my more memorable conversations was with chef Guy Fieri, one of the busiest men in show business and a heck of a nice guy. I finally got him to commit to a time, but I waited at the Starbucks near my mother's place for half an hour, and he never called. I figured he was just too busy, and I left to drive home. On Interstate 405 over Mulholland Drive, my cell rings, and it's Guy.

I needed to think of something quickly, so I pulled off into a residential area, stopped in front of a house and asked if I could call him back in two minutes. I wanted to put him on speaker and record the conversation with my computer, but I couldn't start the audio program, and Garage Band wouldn't open.

I checked for an available Wi-Fi signal, and found the unencrypted network "Joanne" nearby. Angels sang, as I logged onto Skype and called Guy back. I vowed to thank her, so thank you Joanne, whoever you are, and thanks again Guy for a fantastic interview.

Writing this book changed me. It deepened my respect and broadened my perspective relative to what others endure in their lives. My own stage fright seems small compared with that of a firefighter, a heart surgeon, an astronaut and a blind mountain climber. Then again, public speaking is so life-or-death scary for many of these people. We all have performance fears, and if we want to push ourselves to a higher place, we need to improve our skills and mindsets. The rewards are life altering and inspire others who witness our performance growth.

You met Erik Weihenmayer in this book. He lost his eyesight at 13 and became the first blind man to climb Mount Everest and the Seven Summits.

Erik is the bravest dude I've ever met, and he gave me the ultimate validation: "I wish I'd read your book before I went through the Khumbu Icefall."

I have a basic philosophy that I try to uphold whenever I'm conscious enough to just pay attention: Leave people better than when I found them. I want to inspire others to inspire others.

Remember that how you perceive people—and how you think they perceive you—can be deceptive. Before I interviewed him, I watched saxophonist Dave Koz's Hollywood Walk of Fame acceptance speech on YouTube. He's got this natural poise that exudes calm and confidence. I couldn't imagine him ever being scared. I was wrong.

"If it's coming off that way, then I think I'm just lucky and blessed with being able to have the calm exterior. I can pull it together pretty much in any situation. I acquaint my musicianship with my skiing. In other words, I'm really not a good skier, but I can get down any mountain. I can get down, but it might not be pretty."

Knowing Dave as well as I do, this surprised me—he's a great musician. It reminded me that we all have the same vulnerabilities and insecurities, even though we tend to think that other people are somehow immune. It's nice to hear the truth, especially from people we admire. Dave gave me some wonderful feedback about my book and our experience together. "I love what you've done with your career. Any example that you have set and continue to set with how you push yourself into doing these things, you're definitely a leading-edge creator."

What I was really doing was researching the core human drama. Dr. Paul Stoltz told me that on the deck of his ranch on the central California coast. He said, "You're asking really incredible people, 'What do you do, and what have your moments been?' That's a great question to be asking."

This drama is fascinating in its intensity and the lessons it provides. I hope you have found the lessons in this book useful and will use them to propel you forward. Your courage to communicate and act will also move someone else to a better place. You pay it forward, changing the course of history, just by doing a bit of extra work. That makes me happy.

I've learned through experience—and the interviews for this book—that the Three Cs can work at different times in different contexts and at different stages of performance—whatever that performance might be. What's tried and true for one person may be ineffective for another. That's what's so wonderful about the human experience.

AFTERWORD

My wife, Lisa Skarell-Schulman, is a rock. She is beautiful, funny, patient and tolerant. I am often on the road, and when I am home, I frequently do recording sessions, seminars and clinics. Then, I decided to write a book! Lisa, your love is my fuel. Your intelligence and insight added another dimension to this book. I love you; I thank you.

As a survivor of testicular cancer, my chances of ever siring a child were next to none. Zade is a miracle, a bi-lingual, beautiful, dynamic, compassionate, bossy and joyful 5-year-old girl who is learning swimming, yoga, dance and theatre, and has access to her own drum set, percussion, piano and guitar. Zade you are greatest thing on this planet.

My heart overflows with gratitude and love for my parents, Sandy and the late Ben Schulman, my original teachers of tolerance and unconditional love. Many thanks to my brother, Randy Schulman, my musical inspiration who taught me philosophy, production and that it is really OK to be bold and truthful.

Also of inspiration, I express gratitude to my niece, Julie Chang Schulman; David Chang Schul- man, Linda Chang Schulman; Kim Schulman; Hsuan Hua Chang; Gunnar and Karin Skarell; Sarah, David, Alice, Oliver and Max Locke; my godfather and first music teacher, Uncle Ben Greco and his family, Rose, Barbara, Joanne and Mike; and my current family—Sasha Krivtsov and Deon Harvey, Jazz and Ty.

To Stephen Stern, who I met in seventh grade gym class, you are more than a manager and old friend; you are my co-creator of ideas, confidant and counselor.

To my accountant and business manager, Mark Grossman, who I have known since I was 3, I'm grateful and I love you.

Dr. Jim Samuels, no single person on this planet has had a more positive and educational impact on me. After 30 years, you are one of my best friends and my greatest mentor. Your concepts and teachings are the foundation of this book. And thank you for the many great people you introduced me to that are like family: Dr. Jay Klusky, Seth Samuels, Norvin Johnson, Candice Martin and Shirley Izaguirre.

Special thanks to my promotion team: Robert Davidman of Fearless Media and Heather Logrippo of Expose Yourself PR.

Roger King your support as a dear friend and forward thinker has shifted that way I think about myself and my business. Dan Stevens, your comments and endorsement of this book brought tears to my eyes.

Carol Fuchs, you demonstrated solid support and love by hooking me up with your friends, including Vanessa Selbst. Rich Cashman you are the guardian of my family while I'm away. Robert Olshever and Murray Schwartz, thank you for your support and friendship. Steve and Sue Diamond your love and influence from a distance means so much to me. Marlyssa Hart, you are the sister I never had. Christine Zannato, the rekindling of our friendship after so many years has been such a blessing to me, and a special thanks to you for the hook up with Ray Parker Jr.

Julian, Jenn, Jake, Jasper Coryell and Erich, Nannette, Gina and Mia Gobel, you have been our family de facto. Jeff Wallace, Jennifer Kolchier, Tom Conley and Andrew Sokol; you are all lovely friends who helped me develop my seminar presentation, which lead to the creation of this book. Thank you squared! And a special thank you to Sam Gracey, Jenny Smits, Maureen Brooks, Dom Famularo, Bruce Becker, Jill Gurr, Freddie Gruber and Rich Redmond.   To my new friends that are shaping my speaking business with cutting edge thinking, inspiration and action: Bruce Turkel, Shep Hyken, David Etzler, Lynn Rose, Scott Page, Kevin Dunn, Karen Harris and Brian Palmer.

Tim Sanders, you have acknowledged my potential since we met over 10 years ago. You supported me by coming to my speaking gigs and initiated the writing of this book. You inspire forward thinking, calculated action and acknowledgement of spirit. You are a game changer, life changer and the king of gratitude.

And then there's my book team. Many thanks to my editor Jessie States, your involvement in this writing transcends the mere editing of words; I love the way you think. Copy editor Michael Pinchera, I extend my gratitude for your attention to detail and accuracy and your passion for the project. Editor in Chief Gene Stone, the unsung hero, I'm so grateful that you enabled me to actualize a deeper potential. Designer Jason Judy, your patience and willingness to entertain every request and detail in the CLSF visual design is testament to your work ethic. And finally Niseem Soussan of iCreative Advertising- all I can say is WOW!

I am absolutely humbled by the people who have given me their time and intimate thoughts to be part of this book (in alphabetical order by first name): Alan Bean, Baz Halpin, Billy Hayes, Clint Stitser, Dave Koz, David Kalt, Denny Seiwell, Doriana Sanchez, Erik Weihenmayer, Fong Sai U, Fred Grestch, Fred Mossler, Garrett McNamara, Guy Fieri, Jeremy Piven, Jim Samuels, John Baxter, Kelly Gallagher, Kelly Hansen, Kendall Grove, Kevin Goessling, Laura Okmin, Lita Ford, Lucy Streeter, Mark Cenedella, Mark Papia, Matt Glowacki, Paul Stoltz, Phil Carson, Prodigal Sunn, Ray Parker Jr., Robbie Gould, Ronda Beaman, Seb Stella, Sol Ham- burg, Steve Stevens, Stewart Copeland, Tim Sanders, Tony Hsieh, Udo Lindenberg, Vanessa Selbst, Victoria Recaño, Vivian Campbell and Zubin Dimania. Paul Stoltz and Ronda Beaman, your mentoring has shaped my thinking, my speaking career and this book. Alecia Moore, I don't think you realize how your stage performances floor me. Your talent, fearlessness and friendship humble me.

Kelly Gallagher you are a living legend to me; I'm honored to dedicate an entire chapter to you. I love you.

And so many thanks go to my performing and touring families: Roger Davies, Bill Buntain, Nancy Shefts, Nick Cua, Shady Farshadfar, Paul Mirkov- ich, Ollie Marland, Jimmy Slonina, Jenny Douglas Foote, Stacy Campbell, Justin Derrico, Eva Gardner, Jason Chapman, Kat Lucas, Reina Hidalgo, Lori- el Hennington, Tracy Shibata, Janelle Ginestra, Remi Bakkar, Colt Prattes, Khasan Brailsford, John Pelligrinelli, Hannah Hollings, Dane Hoyt, Mark Wise, Dylan Etherington, David Odum, Yvette Beebe, Cole Walister, Mick Jones, Jeff Pilson, Thom Gimbel, Michael Bluestein, Bruce Watson, Robin Ir- vine, Merrie Hart, Mark Bennett and of course Damon Ranger!

I am so fortunate to have the support of my friends in the music gear industry that have supported me with the tools of my trade, foundation of my expression and relationships for life: Fred & Dinah Gretsch, Bob, Winnie, Andy, Billy & Sally Zildjian, Vic, Kelly & Tracy Firth, Remo Belli, Mark Nel- son, John Palmer, Ken Fredenberg, Brent Barnett, Don & Chris Lombardi, Juels Thomas, Mike Nieland, Terry Tlatelpa-Lopez, Peter Stairs, Chris Stan- kee, Ann McNally, Mark Love, Shirlene Lau, Katie Bursey, Bob Rupp, Joe Tes- ta, Ben Davies, Marco Soccoli, Adam Murphy, Chris Hart, Ryan Smith, Pierre Morant, the GC team: Glenn Noyes, Ray Brych and Ryan Carr.

…and finally to Ringo and Buddy…

CONQUERING LIFE'S STAGE FRIGHT

STAGE FRIGHT

THREE STEPS TO TOP PERFORMANCE

BY MARK SCHULMAN